NINTENDO 64 POCKET POWER GUIDE
UNAUTHORIZED VOLUME 3

Prima Publishing
Rocklin, California
(916) 632-4400
www.primagames.com

Created by:
Prima Creative Services, England
Managing Editor: Nick Roberts

CONTENTS

Important:

ISBN: 7615-1465-1
Library of Congress Catalog Card Nu
Printed in the United States of Americ

98 99 00 01 HH 10 9 8 7 6 5 4 3 2

AEROFIGHTERS ASSAULT
SECRETS
Enable Spanky

To switch on Spanky, you must complete all of the game's bonus missions. The next time you start up, he'll be waiting!

Enable Mao Mao

Go to the title screen and press: **C(L), C(D), C(R), C(U), C(L), C(R), C(D)**. Now Mao Mao is available.

New Paint Job

In either the Main Game or Boss Attack modes, press the **Right shoulder** button on the plane selection screen and you get a shiny new paint job for your mean machine. If you're playing in Death Match mode, you must press the **Right shoulder button** as you select your plane to get this cheat to work.

This secret only works on the four original planes.

Enemies in Death Match

Death Match mode is nothing unless you build up a collection of enemies to defeat. Each time you complete a level, you add another enemy to Death Match mode. There are six to find.

FIND THE BONUS STAGES
Air Docking

The bonus stage here is earned when you complete both the Tokyo and Pacific Ocean stages with an impressive high score.

Shuttle Defense

There's a shuttle to be saved—if you're quick enough! Again, you must complete the Tokyo and Pacific Ocean stages, but also Air Battle, too—and in lightning-fast time! If you reach the Desert stage and the sun is setting, you're too late to play this bonus stage.

Goliath Defense

You must have completed the first two bonus stages before you can proceed to this one. It is played after Fortress.

Secret Stage

If you are talented enough to complete all seven regular stages, then go on to complete the three bonus stages, there is a secret stage waiting for you. It's found after you finish the Ice Cave stage.

WINGMAN TALENTS

When you select your plane for a mission, three other planes accompany you as your wingmen. These aircraft are essential, as they engage an enemy plane each, leaving you free to concentrate on doing the job in hand.

You can activate the talents of a plane when required by simply attacking the same enemy as they are tailing. You can only do this once per stage, however. The talents are....

A-10: Attacking the boss
F-14: Defending the team
FSX: Defending the player
SU-35: Defending the team

SPECIAL MANUEVERS

Each plane has special maneuvers that you can use to get out of tricky situations, or simply to give the enemy a bit of a surprise!

FSX/SU-35
Cobra
Pull back on the analog joystick and press **C(D)**. Now pull back on the joystick again and press **C(U)**. This must be done quite quickly. Get it right and your speed drops and your flight path changes.

Culbit backflip
Pull back on the analog joystick and press **C(D)**. Now pull back on the joystick again and press **C(U)**, but continue to hold the joystick down. Again, speed is important. Make sure you don't perform this move too close to the ground!

F-14/A-10/F-15
Rudder reversal
Decrease the speed of your plane and pull back on the joystick until the nose is at 30°. Now tap twice on either **C(L)** or **C(R)** to make a hard turn in that direction. The plane won't perform the move if the nose is not at 30°, so adjust the elevation and try again.

BOMBERMAN 64
SKILLS

Kicking bombs

By dropping a bomb with **A** then pressing the button again, Bomberman kicks the bomb in the direction he's facing. This is a good way of attacking enemies at long range—Bomberman can stay well away from the blast zone. This technique is also used for blasting out-of-reach areas.

Expanding bombs

Pick up any bomb and repeatedly press the **A** button and it expands. When it has expanded as far as it will go, the bomb shines for a second. It is now a Pumped Up bomb!

These have a much larger blast zone, so you can kill more enemies at one time. Many blocks in the game can only be destroyed with Pumped bombs.

Bomb stairways

Once you have collected the Remote bomb power-up, you can use your bombs to help you out of tricky situations. As long as you don't detonate them when Bomberman is nearby, they can be used as stairways! It's a simple matter of creating bombs of different sizes and throwing them into a stairway shape— Bomberman can then bounce along them!

Bouncing bombs

If Bomberman needs to blast a pillar but it's out of range, he can use Remote bombs to bounce others far enough to reach the target.

POWER-UPS
Blue Bomb

Bomberman starts with a basic bomb in his arsenal, but he can only drop two at a time. Picking up a blue Bomb power-up increases the number of bombs he's able to drop at once by a unit, to a maximum of eight bombs.

Fire

The basic bomb can do serious damage at close range, but you sometimes need an explosion to cover a larger area. Each time you pick up a Fire power-up, the explosion area increases—up to a set maximum, of course.

Heart

The Heart is one of the more useful power-ups. Pick it up and Bomberman carries it with him at all times. If he's fatally wounded by an enemy, instead of losing a life,

Bomberman loses the heart and can continue his adventure. The great thing is that the Heart simply bounces a short distance away—if Bomberman runs after it, he can collect it again!

Power

A red bomb inside a yellow flash is a Power item. This increases the power of the bombs carried by Bomberman from black to red. A red bomb covers a much larger surface area when detonated, and has the power to destroy the large blue blocks found around some stages.

Remote

Regardless of the kind of bomb Bomberman is carrying, picking up a heart with a black bomb inside it makes those bombs remote-controlled. This adds a lot more stability to bombs, as they're detonated with the Z button, instead of being automatically triggered on a timer.

Blue Diamond

All games have their throwaway power-ups. In *Bomberman 64*, they're diamonds. These are littered everywhere. Picking up a blue diamond adds one diamond point to your total. Collect 50 and you earn an extra life.

Red Diamond

The red diamonds work in exactly the same way as the blue ones, but they add five diamond points to the total instead of a miserly single point.

Gold Card

Five Gold Cards are hidden in each stage and Bomberman must perform specific tasks to earn them. The locations of these cards are given in detail in the stage solutions.

Collect them all and a nice surprise may be waiting!

Costume Pieces

If you thought the gold cards were rare, you haven't tried looking for costume pieces! Collecting these gives you the option of customizing your Bomberman in a multi-player game. A costume piece power-up is a "?" on a small ball. A red one gives a head costume piece, green protects your arms, blue covers your body, and yellow gives leg pieces.

CHAMELEON TWIST
HINTS AND TIPS

1. Go north from your start point and speak to the creature in front of you for some advice. Continue north, where you find a small golden crown, so grab it. Now go to the west, where you find a small tree—a second crown is hidden beneath the foliage. With this collected, head north and go up the steps.

2. Here you see a small heart pick-up, so jump up and grab it— this gives your life gauge a boost! Continue north and you're confronted by a group of small spiky hedgehogs—simply use your tongue to destroy them. Now to the west is another golden crown, so walk over and grab it.

3. Follow the path and before long you reach a section that features four posts—two on your side of a gap, two on the other. You must use your tongue to latch onto a distant post and get across safely. Continue to follow the thin path along the side of the cliff—take extra care here as falling off results in instant death!

4. You have to get across large gaps in the path by once again using your tongue as a kind of bridge—this is where the practice you had a moment ago is useful, as falling from here

means death. When you reach a water-filled section, you must move from leaf to leaf using the posts and your tongue. On the final leaf you find another golden crown, so grab it!

5. Continue following the path deeper into the level. Once again, take care, as the path is extremely thin and falling off kills the chameleon! Before long you find a hollow tree trunk. Use this to jump up onto the nearby platform and grab the heart.

6. Now walk up the tree trunk that is directly in front of the heart you have just collected. At the top of this you'll find a golden crown—take care, as falling off this trunk spells death! Now retrace your steps to the hollow tree trunk on the main path. Walk into this to find another crown.

7. Follow the path until you reach a thin log that spans a small pit. In the pit are two hedgehogs and a crown. Jump down and quickly kill the hedgehogs before grabbing the crown. With this done, jump up and use your tongue to grab onto the post and get out of the pit safely. Now continue to follow the path to the east.

CLAYFIGHTER 63 1/3
SPECIAL MOVES

BAD MR FROSTY
Snowball	hold ←, →+Punch
Pickaxe	↓, ↘, →, Punch
Vertical Pickaxe	↓, ↓+Punch

Ice Splash ....↓, ↙, ←+Punch
Snow Blower ....hold ←, →+Kick
Blizzard Kick ....→, ↓, ↘+Kick
Stomp..←+C(R)
Taunt...L shoulder+R shoulder+A or B

Super Moves

Blizzard Combo........................↓, ↘, →, ↓, ↘, →+Kick
Spin Kicks ....→, ↘, ↓, ↙, ←, →+Kick
Sub-Zero......................................↓, ↙, ←, ←, ↙, ↓, ↘, →+Kick

Claytalities

Ice Hammer................................↓, ←, ↓, ← (close)
Belly Boot ....→, ↓, ←, ← (close)
Launch Kick...............................↓, ↓, R shoulder+ L shoulder (close)
Magic Hat.....................................R shoulder, ←, ↓, ↓, →; or hold R
                    shoulder, ↓, ↓, → (close)
Polar Bearhug ....←, ↓, ↓, →, L shoulder (close)

Combo

11-hit..hold ←, →+C(R), C(D), →, ↘,
                    ↓+C(D), A, ↓, ↙, ←+Punch

Enders

↓, ↙, ←+Punch
→, ↓, ↘+C(D) or C(R)

BLOB

Sawblade.......................................hold ←, →+Punch
Cannonball..................................↓, ↙, ←+Punch
Punches ....←, ↓, ↙+Punch
Glove..→, ↓, ↘+Punch
Nose-dive ....→, ↘, ↓, ↙, ←+Kick
Mallet...hold ←, →+Kick
Auto Run ....→, hold →
Jaw Break ....↓, ↓+C(U)
Taunt...L shoulder+R shoulder+A
Flag...L shoulder+R shoulder+C(D)
Combo Breaker........................→, ↓, →+Punch

Super Moves

Dashing Punches.......................↓, ↘, →, ↓, ↘, →+Punch
Axe Jump ....↓, ↙, ←, ↓, ↙, ←+Punch
Axe Spin ....↓, ↙, ←, ↓, ↙, ←+Kick

Claytalities

Eat ....↓, ↓, ↓, L shoulder (close)
Inflate...↓, ↓, →, →, ↓ (sweep)

Lobe Bite	L shoulder, ↓, ↓, →, R (close)
Mallet	↓, ↘, →+R shoulder (close)
Missile	←, ↓, →, R shoulder (close)
Shattered	L shoulder, R shoulder, ↓, ↓ (close)
Tank	↓, ↓, ←, →, C(U) (screen)

Combos

Four-hit	hold ←, C(R), →+C(R), C(R)
Eight-hit	hold ←, →+ C(R), C(D), →, ↓, ↘+ C(D)

Enders

↓, ↙, ←+Punch

→, ↓, ↘+Kick

BONKER

Clay Cat	↓, ↘, →+Punch
Ferris Wheel	↓, ↘, →+Kick
Merry-Go-Clown	↓, ↙, ←+Kick
Dash	hold ←, →+Punch
Turning Kick	hold ←, →+Kick
Hammer	↓, ↓+Punch
Taunt	L shoulder +R shoulder+A

Super Moves

Bestiary	↓, ↘, →, ↓, ↘, →+Punch
Cartwheel	↓, ↘, →, ↓, ↘, →+Kick
Spinning Kicks	↓, ↙, ←, ↓, ↙, ←+Kick

Claytalities

Butt ....→, →, → (close)
Cannonball...........................↓, ↓, ↓, ↓ (sweep)
Keg ....→, ↓, → (sweep)
Flip Flop ....→, ←, ←, → (close)

Combo

Nine-hit ....hold ←, →+C(R), C(D), ↓, ↘, →, ↓,
↘, →+Kick

BOOGERMAN

Booger...................................↓, ↘, →+Punch
Slide ....hold ←, →+Kick
Gas Slide ....↓, ↙, ←+Kick
Jumping Gas Slide...............↓, ↙, ←+Kick, while in air
Turning Kick........................hold ↓, ←+Kick
Chest Shot............................↓+C(U), while jumping forward
Above Suspicion ....↓, ↓+Punch
Taunt....................................L shoulder+R shoulder+A

Super Moves

Belch.....................................↓, ↘, →, ↓, ↘, →+Punch
Slide ....↓, ↙, ←, ↓, ↙, ←+Punch
Gas Engine...........................↓, ↙, ←, ↓, ↙, ←+Kick

Claytalities

Belch.....................................↓, ↓, ↓, R shoulder (close)
Black Out..............................↓, →, ↓, L shoulder (sweep)
Turbo....................................→, ←, ↓, ←, →, L shoulder (close)
Fiery......................................↓, ↓, ←, ←, →, →, R shoulder (sweep)
Dumper.................................↓, ↓, ←, ←, C(L) (screen)
Turning Kick.........................←, →, ↓, ↓, R shoulder (close)

Combos

Five/six-hit............................jump+C(D), ↓, ↙, ←+A
Nine-hit ....hold ←, →+C(R), C(D), →, ↓, ↘+C(D)

Enders

←, ↓, ↙+Punch
→, ↓, ↘+Kick

DR KILN

Charge ....hold ←, →, Punch
Fire Shot...............................↓, ↘, →+Punch
Electric Charge ....→, ↓, ↘+Punch
Slide ....↓, ↘, →+Kick
Spinning Kick ....hold ←, →+Kick

Pogostick Kick............................↓, ↓, Kick
Taunt..L shoulder+R shoulder+A
Combo Breaker..........................→, ↓, ↘+Punch

Super Moves

Gunshot ....↓, ↘, →, ↓, ↘, →+Punch
Slider..↓, ↘, →, ↓, ↘, →+Kick

Claytalities

Belly Cut ....→, →, → (close)
Big Throw....................................↓, →, ←, → (close)
Blow Up ....↓, ↓, ↓ (sweep)
Internal Exam............................←, ↓, ↓, → (sweep)

Combos

Four-hit.......................................↓, ↘, →, ↓, ↘, →+Punch, B (corner only)
11-hit...hold ←, →+C(U), C(D), →, ↘,
                ↓+C(U), ↓, ↘, →, ↓, ↘, →+C(U)
15-hit...hold ←, →+C(R), C(D), →, ↘,
                ↓+C(R), ↓, ↘, →, ↓, ↘, →+C(R)

EARTHWORM JIM

Run Punch ....hold ←, →+Punch
Uppercut......................................→, ↓, ↘+Punch
Laser Shot...................................↓, ↘, →+Punch
Air Dive.......................................↓, ↘, →+Kick
Roll...↓, ↓+Kick
Head Punch................................↘+C(U)
Overhead.....................................↓, ↓+Punch
Taunt..L shoulder+R shoulder+Kick

Super Moves

Laser Blast ....↓, ↘, →, ↓, ↘, →+Punch
Max Air ....↓, ↙, ←, ↓, ↙, ←+Punch
Uppercuts....................................↓, ↘, →, ↓, ↘, →+Kick
Wormlash ....↓, ↙, ←, ↓, ↙, ←+Kick

Claytalities

Uppercut......................................←, ↓, →, R shoulder (close)
Cow Season................................↓, ↓, ↓, L shoulder+
                R shoulder (half screen)
Swell Head...................................↓, →, ←, ←, L shoulder (close)
Super Kick...................................↓, ↓, ←, ←, →, →, R shoulder (close)
Splat...←, →, →, →, R shoulder (close)

Combos

Eight-hit.......................................hold ←, →+C(U), C(D), →, ↓,
                ↘+C(U)

Enders

→, ↓, ↘+C(L) or C(U)

←, ↓, ↙+C(D) or C(R)

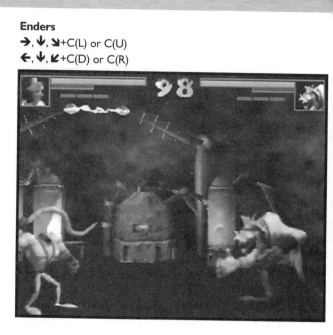

HOUNGAN

Chicken Fling	↓, ↘, →+Punch
Finger Walk	←, →+Punch
Hit and Run	hold ←, →+Kick
Hover	↓, ↙, ←+Kick (also during jump)
Hover Kicks	→, ↓, ↘+Kick
Dive	↓, ↓+Kick, during jump
Above and Beyond	hold ↓, ↓+C(U)
Taunt	L shoulder+R shoulder+A or B
Combo Breaker	→, ↓, ↘+Kick

Super Moves

Chicken	↓, ↘, →, ↓, ↘, →+Punch
Spin Attack	↓, ↙, ←, ↓, ↙, ←+Kick
Handy	→, ↘, ↓, ↙, ←+Punch

Claytalities

Solidify/Melt	L shoulder (sweep)
Voodoo	←, ↓, →+L shoulder (half screen)
Fowl Play	↓, ↘, →, ↘, ↓ (sweep)
Big Hands	↓, ↓, →, ←+R shoulder (sweep)

Combo

10-hit	hold ←, →+C(R), C(D), ↓, ↘, →+Punch

Enders

↓, ↘, →+Punch

↓, ↘, →+Kick

ICKYBOD CLAY

Head Shot	↓, ↘, →, Punch
Bat Attack	←, ↓, ↙+Punch (button affects angle)
Spinning Wheel	hold ←, →+Punch
Vertical Wheel	→, ↘, ↓, ↙, ←+C(L)
Uppercut	→, ↓, ↘+Punch
Teleport	→, ↓, ↘+Kick
Spook Shoulder	hold ←, →, Kick
	(also in air, timing affects angle)
Clay Compendium	←, ↙, ↓, ↘, →+C(D)
Bod Above	↓, ↓, C(U)
Taunt	L shoulder+R shoulder+B
Combo Breaker	hold ←, →+Kick

Super Moves

Scary	↓, ↘, →, ↓, ↘, →+Kick
Teleport Combo	→, →, ←, ←+Kick
Invisible Throw	↓, ↙, ←, ↓, ↙, ←+B (close)

Claytalities

Eddy Spin	←, ↙, ↓, ↘, →+L shoulder
	(half screen)
Let's Puncharty	↓, ↓, →, ←+R shoulder (half screen)

Combos

Three-hit	throw with →+C(D), jump C(D), →, ↓, ↘+C(U)
Six-hit	C(D), ←, ↙, ↓, ↘, →+C(D)
10-hit	↓, ↘, →, ↓, ↘, →+Kick, C(R), C(R) (corner only)
11-hit	jump, C(R), C(R), ↓, ↘, →, ↓, ↘, →+C(R)

Enders

↓, ↘, →+Punch

↓, ↘, →+Kick

KUNG POW

Monkey Man	↓, ↘, →+Punch
Pan Hit	hold ←, →+Punch
Slap	↓, ↙, ←+Punch
Side Kick	↓, ↘, →+Kick

Uppercut Kick .... →, ↓, ↘+Kick
Dash Kick .... hold ←, →+Kick
Crawler .... →, ↘, ↓, ↙, ←+Kick
Diving Kick .... ↓+C(R), during jump
Ghost Kick .... →+C(R)
Kung Fly .... ↓, ↓+Punch
Taunt .... L shoulder+R shoulder+A
Combo Breaker .... →, ↓, ↘+Kick

Super Moves

Multi-kick .... ↓, ↘, →, ↓, ↘, →+Kick
Kick Chopper .... ↓, ↙, ←, ↓, ↙, ←+Kick
Knife Attack .... jump, ↓, ↘, →, ↓, ↘, →+Punch

Claytalities

Karate Chop .... ↓, ↓, →, → (close)
Stamina Stamp .... ↓, ↓, ↓ (sweep)
Clay Chop .... →, →, → (sweep)
Pan Throw .... →, ↓, ←, ↓ (half screen)

Combos

Five-hit .... jump, B, B, B,A, →, ↓, ↘+A
29-hit .... hold ←, →+C(R), C(D), →, ↘,
↓+C(R), ↓, ↙, ←, ↓, ↙, ←+C(R)

SUMO SANTA

Friendly Hug .... ←, →+Punch
Belly Butt .... →, ↓, ↘+Punch
Throw Gift .... ↓, ↘, →+Punch
Step Kick .... hold ←, →+Kick
Splat .... hold ↓, →+Punch
Cane and Able .... ↓, ↓, C(U)
Taunt .... L shoulder+R shoulder+A

Super Moves

Tub Thumpin' .... ↓, ↘, →, ↓, ↘, →+Punch
Bicycle Kick .... ↓, ↘, →, ↓, ↘, →+Kick
Great Stamp .... ←, ←, →, →, Kick

Claytalities

Doubler .... ←, ←, →, ← (sweep)
Impact .... ↓, ↓, ↓, R shoulder (sweep)

Combos

Eight-hit .... hold ←, →+C(R), C(D), ↓, ↘, →+Kick
12-hit .... jump, C(L), C(L), ↓, ↘, →, ↓, ↘,
→+C(U)

Enders

↓, ↘, →+Punch
↓, ↘, →+Kick

TAFFY

Gumball	↓, ↘, →+Punch
Curveball	→, ↘, ↓, ↙, ←+Kick
	(button affects angle)
Twister	↓, ↙, ←+Punch (also in air)
Roll	hold ←, →+Punch
Cartwheel	hold ←, →+Kick
Punt	↘+C(R)
Rear Throw	←+Punch (close)
High Chop	↓, ↓+C(L)
Taunt	L shoulder+R shoulder+Punch
	(button affects speed)
Combo Breaker	↓, ↙, ←+Punch

Super Moves

Twister 2	↓, ↙, ←, ↓, ↙, ←+Punch
Kicking Candy	↓, ↓, ←, ←+Kick
Machine Gun	hold Punch, Kick

Claytalities

Taffy Twins	↓, ↘, →+R (close)
Roll	L shoulder, R shoulder, L shoulder,
	R shoulder (screen)
Gumball	↓, ↓, →, →, R (sweep)
Throw Gumball	←, →, ←, → (sweep)

Combos

Four-hit	jump + C(R), then ↓, ↙, ←+C(U)
Five-hit	hold →+Kick, ↓+A
Seven-hit	hold ←, →+C(R), C(D), ↓, ↘, →+Kick

Enders

↓, ↘, →+Punch
↓, ↘, →+Kick

T. HOPPY

Jack Punch	→, ↓, ↘+Punch
Run and Punch	hold ←, →+Punch
Shock Move	←, ↙, ↓, ↘, →+C(L) (throws if close)
Bunny Bash	→, →+B or A
Super Slap	↓, ↘, →+C(D) or C(R) (close)
Spring Kick	←, ↓, ↙+Kick
Stamp	hold ↓, →+Kick

Hop and Punch ....↓, ↓, C(U)

Taunt...................................L shoulder+R shoulder+A

Combo Breaker......................→, ↓, ↘+Punch

Super Moves

Turbo Uppercut......................↓, ↘, →, ↓, ↘, →+Punch

Lucky Shots...........................↓, ↙, ←, ↓, ↙, ←+Punch

Super Rabbit Punch ....↓, ↘, →, ↓, ↘, →+Kick (close)

Claytalities

Stamp ....→, →, →, → (close)

Magic .... ←, ←, →, →, R shoulder (sweep)

Carrot.................................→, ↓, ←, L shoulder (close)

Combos

Four-hit...............................A, A, →, →+A

Four-hit...............................jump, C(R), C(R), ↓, ↘, →, ↓, ↘,
→+C(R), dash, →, ↓, ↘+C(U)

Eight-hit ....←, ↙, ↓, ↘, →+C(L), B, ↓, ↘,
→+Punch

Eight-hit ....hold ←, →+C(R), C(D), ↓, ↘, →+Kick

Nine-hit ....jump, C(R), C(R), ↓, ↘, →, ↓, ↘,
→+Punch

Enders

↓, ↘, →+Punch

↓, ↘, →+Kick

CHEATS

Character Color

When you select your fighter, use **C(D)** and they'll have a
different-colored costume—or body, depending on the character!

Background Select

This is for a two-player game. When the "versus" screen is
displayed, simply press **C(R)** and **C(L)** to find the name of the
background you want to fight against. If you're playing against
the CPU....

Secret Options

If you want more variety to your fights, hold the **Left shoulder**
button and press **C(U), C(R), C(L), C(D), B, A, A** at the
character selection screen. It flashes when you do this correctly.
Go to the Option menu and choose the new Secret Options
menu, where among other things you can change the fighters'
voices, switch off the Claytality timer, set the game's speed, and,

yes, allow a single player to choose a background! As before, use **C(R)** and **C(L)** buttons on the "versus" screen.

Play as Boogerman

Make your opponents afraid of the Boogerman. At the character selection screen, hold the **Left shoulder** button and press **Up, Right, Down, Left, Right, Left** on the joypad. The screen flashes and his face appears at the bottom of the screen

Play as Dr. Kiln

To play as Dr. Kiln, go to the character selection screen. Press and hold the **Left shoulder** button while you press **B, C(L), C(U), C(R), C(D), A**. The screen flashes if the Dr. Kiln cheat has operated and he appears in the selection grid.

Play as Sumo Santa

To gain this crazed Claus, go to the character selection screen, hold the **Left shoulder** and press **A, C(D), C(R), C(U), C(L), B**. The screen flashes and Santa's ready to go!

Random Character Selection

Can't decide who to control? While at the character selection screen, hold the **Left shoulder** and **Right shoulder** buttons to select one at random.

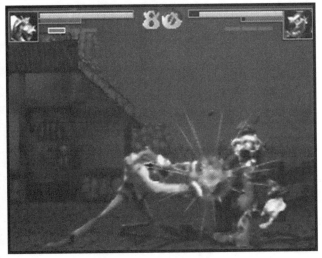

DIDDY KONG RACING
MULTIPLAYER HINTS, TIPS, AND STRATEGIES

Diddy Kong Racing features 20 multiplayer tracks, five in each of four worlds—Dino Domain, Sherbet Island, Snowflake Mountain, and Dragon Forest. The only way to access them all is by playing completely through Adventure mode.

Completing Adventure mode unlocks all the multiplayer tracks. You may select any available track for multiplayer action. In addition, a Trophy Race available in each of the four worlds combines the first four tracks of each world into a grand prix.

Read this section carefully. The multiplayer hints, tips, and strategies we discuss in this section hold true for all 20 tracks available in Multiplayer mode. Having this information at your instant disposal can spell the difference between a glorious victory and a humbling defeat.

Drive Offensively

We can sum up the basic, uncomplicated difference between Adventure mode and Multiplayer mode in *Diddy Kong Racing* in three words—offense versus defense. In Adventure mode you must drive defensively, concentrating all your efforts on completing the race having accomplished all your goals. In Multiplayer mode, you must drive offensively, focusing on upsetting, disturbing, hindering, and otherwise interfering with your opponents' runs for the finish line, at the same time avoiding their efforts to prevent you from winning. That's all there is to it—but there's big fun to be had in that one "small" difference!

Bananas

If we were going to make a list of absolutely unbreakable rules for winning in Multiplayer mode, the first would be: "Always collect 10 Bananas as fast as you can—and try your best to keep them!" So what happens when you collect 10 Bananas? The second you pick up the tenth Banana, your character's vehicle instantly upgrades—better speed, better handling, better performance all the way around. And although better top speed is a great benefit, it's better handling that will win race after race.

Better handling means simply this: When you're speeding around a sharp turn, your opponent, who perhaps has only seven Bananas, will slide into the wall and lose a few seconds. Meanwhile, you, the smart racer with 10 Bananas (or more), will stick the turn without fishtailing all over the road, putting you several seconds ahead of your opponent. Multiply those few extra seconds by the number of curves on the track and it's easy to see why better handling wins races.

But don't even think about stopping at just 10 Bananas. You'll need as many Bananas as you can possibly collect. This not only prevents the other racers from getting 10 Bananas, too, but protects you in case the racer behind you gets off a lucky shot that costs you a couple of Bananas. Make sure you have a few Bananas to spare, so you're not in danger of losing your competitive edge.

TIPS

● If you get 10 Multifire Missiles but don't use them all (leave at least one unused), the next time you burst a Red Balloon (without running over a different colored Balloon first) you'll reacquire all 10!

● If both you and your opponent have Magnets of the same color, and if you both trigger those Magnets at the same time, the Magnets will repel—flinging the two of you in opposite directions and costing precious time! Only Magnets of different colors attract each other.

● Remember: Take your finger off the A button just before you pass over a Zipper! You always get a longer, more powerful Speed Boost if you're not mashing the A button as you pass over a Zipper. You can hit the A button to accelerate again when you see and hear the Speed Boost begin to diminish.

● At the start of the race, tap the A button quickly several times a split second before the announcer says "Go!" to get a quick Speed Boost, putting you out ahead of the pack!

● If you're driving a Car, hit the shoulder button while turning to power slide around a corner.

This controlled skid helps keep your Car facing the right direction, saving you time. A second here and a second there really add up over the course of the game.

● If you're driving the Hovercraft, be ready to tap the shoulder button when you're going up a slope. This pops you up in the air and flings you forward, possibly even leapfrogging you up and over the racer ahead!

DUKE NUKEM 64
WEAPONS

Duke's "Mighty Foot"— Always loaded
Snubbed by some as a weapon of last resort, Duke's steel-toed army boots have tactical uses. A swift kick to nonthreatening objects or even the weakest of enemies will get the job done and save precious ammo to boot. If your arsenal is running low, open inanimate objects like garbage cans with a kick, but mainly after you have cleared the area of Alien scum. Vitamin X gives you a power kick, but even under normal use, holding down the fire button gives Duke a karate-action effect.

Pistol—12 shots per clip; 192 max.
Duke's standard-issue sidearm is a pea-shooter with a purpose. It takes a few rounds to take out even the weakest Aliens, except at point-blank range. But depressing the trigger will give you rapid fire—until your clip runs out, that is. Aside from its poor effectiveness, it also requires frequent and agonizing reload pauses. Use on objects to save the serious ammo, or to assassinate from behind. Occasionally, you will run into dumdums, supercharged clips that give the pistol more the kick of a shotgun.

Shotgun—10 rounds per shell box; 50 max.
Ka-chung, ka-chung, bang! Ah, Duke's official soundtrack. Might as well give it a name, because this baby will be your closest friend for the duration. It is a pump-action avenger that reloads quickly and can take out low-level Aliens in one shot. It dices Enforcers

and Octabrains pretty well, too. Less precise at longer ranges, but forgiving of bad aim in close quarters, it's your weapon of choice in mid-sized to small rooms. Check your ammo type, though, because loading explosive shells in this gun will give you a kick in the head if you are too close. Otherwise, it transforms the shotgun into a dream weapon.

SMGs: Sub-Machine Guns—100 rounds per SMG ammo; 400 max.

This excellent rapid-fire weapon will erase most Aliens and even Pig Cops and Enforcers in a second or two. Superb for strafing small rooms filled with Alien hordes or a nest of slime. Use shorter bursts rather than continuous fire to conserve the 400 rounds.

Grenade Launcher—12 rounds per grenade box; 48 max.

Consider this a deadly billiard ball. Its delayed action and rubbery bounce make it as much of a menace to you as to walls and baddies. The canisters from this beauty can take out a wall and decapitate most enemies, but they tend to bounce off walls and blow up in your own face if you fail to take precautions. Grenades often explode on impact when they hit a fleshy target or the weak part of a wall. Otherwise, use ricochet strategies to slow the canister down enough to reach its hard target.

Pipe Bombs—5 bombs per pack; 50 max.

The sneakiest weapon in your arsenal and the all-purpose explosive for times when you do not want to be near the blast. Toss one or more through an unexplored door, into water, or in the path of an oncoming meanie. Impress your friends by planting one in an elevator and sending it up to greet any welcoming party above.

Shrinker/Expander—6 rounds per shrinker crystal; 66 max./33 rounds per expander crystal: 99 max.

Moderately effective after a good deal of experience, but always a lot of fun to use, this weapon has varying effects on different Aliens. The green-colored shooter literally shrinks low- and mid-level baddies, such as Enforcers and Pig Cops, so that Duke can exercise his "Mighty Foot" on them. On upper-level creatures and most inanimate objects, such as turrets, it is a waste of time. The expander may be more fun. It expands some folks until they

burst. One warning: Some blossoming beasts, such as Enforcers, give off shrapnel and can take you out with them. Try one of these on the much-despised Alien Commanders.

Missile Launcher—5 rounds per missile pack; 50 max.
Kills Aliens dead on contact or your money back. This very powerful weapon is great for clearing out a room that you are about to enter or the end of longer hallways. For pesky Sentry Drones, this is the weapon of choice, as it shows some neat homing capabilities, especially when it gets some heat-seeking missiles in later missions. The blast range also is very forgiving of poor aim—unless you hit something close to you, of course.

Laser Tripbombs—I per pickup; 10 max.
Set 'em and forget 'em. Plant these booby traps across hallways and doorways to surprise pursuing baddies. Good for using at unexplored but noisy doorways and even as a variation on the pipe-bomb elevator trick. If you have a major snarler closed in somewhere, place several along the door and then lure the thing into his doom. But don't forget where you planted them. It takes an explosive to set them off from a safe distance.

Plasma Cannon—33 rounds per plasma pack; 99 max.
Like the shrinker/expander, this often can be prettier than it is effective. It has variable destructive capacity, according to how long you keep the trigger depressed before releasing. It runs out of juice quickly, so reserve it for tough spots. As the glowing plasma at the end of the barrel turns from gooey green to hot blue, the plasma cannon's punch increases. Hold it down for five or more seconds, and you can take out a full room. Good for shooting down a long hallway or through an open door or window. It vaporizes rather than explodes objects, so it is good for Drones and especially fine as an anti-Battlelord device.

CHEAT MENU
There is a secret cheat menu hidden away inside the game. Go to the main menu screen and press **Left, Left, L, L, Right, Right,**

Left, Left. L is the left shoulder button and Left is left on the D-pad. The cheat menu will instantly appear on the screen for you to select exciting items from. With this done you can also access the following cheats with extra button combinations...

Fountain of Youth
You can get yourself unlimited health restoring power-ups with this clever little trick. Simply blow up anything water related: a toilet, fire hydrant, or water fountain is ideal. Now walk up to the water gushing out and hold down the **A** button—your health will magically be restored.

Level Select
Again, with the Cheat Menu code already active press **L, L, L, C(R), Right, Left, Left, C(L)**. The cheat options will now include a level select too!

No Monsters
You can also switch the monsters in the game on and off by accessing the Cheat Menu and then pressing **L, C(L), Left, R, C(R), Right, Left, Left, Right**. A siren will sound if you have been successful.

All Items
After inputting the Cheat Meny code return to the main menu screen and press **R, C(R), Right, L, C(L), Left, C(R), Right**. A new option will now appear for you to have all items on when you start a game. Novices to the first-person 3-D shooter genre will want to make the first few tips below habitual. They are the tried-and-true lessons of survival in this kind of game. But even shooter vets will want to review the later tips for Duke-specific material.

Invincibility
After entering the Cheat Menu code press the **Right shoulder** button seven times followed by **Left** on the D-pad. You should hear a tone if you have done it right, indicating that invincibility is on on the cheat menu!

EXTREME-G
CHEATS

Extreme-G has a large and varied selection of cheat codes. To use them, enter the "Extreme Contest" and press the **Right shoulder** button on the bike selection screen. Choose the "Name" option and enter your chosen code (remember, Right shoulder switches between upper and lower case letters). If it's entered correctly, you hear a sound when you press **Start**. Remember that more than one code can be active at the same time. If you want to cancel a code, enter it again.

Infinite Weaponry
To sample all of the weapons, use the name arsenal. You automatically get a new weapon every few seconds.

Infinite Turbos
If you keep finding yourself near the bottom of the rankings, an infinite amount of turbo boosts will help. Enter the nitroid code to get them.

Easy Victories
Use the code RA50 and if you quit a race, the game believes you completed the race at the same ranking. This means if you can pull ahead of the pack, if only briefly, you can quit and instantly win the race!

Slippery Tracks
If you're finding *Extreme-G* too easy, make the tracks more difficult with the banana code. The slippery road surface makes cornering very difficult.

Extreme Speed
Should Extreme-G feel too slow, even when using turbo boosts, input xtreme. The game moves even faster!

Translucent Scenery
Barriers and the track itself turn translucent if you use ghostly as

your name. Spooky!

Stealth Mode
If you input the stealth code, all the vehicles are invisible! It isn't as confusing as it sounds, because their shadows and weapons can still be seen.

Upside Down
Enter antigrav and the tracks are inverted. At least the displays are the right way up....

Boulder Bike
To rumble along the tracks as a huge boulder, use roller as your cheat code.

Programmers' Bikes
If you input **XGTEAM** then use the first name of any of the programming team, their face appears on the back of your bike. Look at the credits to learn the names, but here are a few to get you started: **SHAWN, JUSTIN, JOHN, GREG**.

Shoot Fergus
FERGUS is the name of the programming company's director, and if you use his name, the shoot-'em-up target drones turn into his face.

Magnify Mode
To shift the viewpoint, so that your bike is squashing at the bottom of the screen and scenery looms above you, enter magnify as your cheat code.

Fish Eye Lens
To distort the game, as if viewed through a fish eye lens, use the word fisheye as your name. The scenery is stretched out and you're vehicle's in the middle distance—things seem to zoom past even quicker!

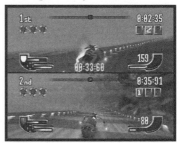

Ugly Mode
To switch off the N64's graphics smoothing

technology, enter uglymode for a PlayStation-style pixelated courses.

Wire-frame Graphics

To remove the textures, use wired as your cheat code. Only wire-frame graphics remain!

F1 POLE POSITION 64
BASIC TACTICS

- Lose your car's nose cone and your speed increases without reducing the handling performance. Knock pieces such as the cone or rear fin from an opponent's cars and they usually go into the pits on next lap.
- Don't throw your car too heavily over the track edge—it damages the car's suspension. The occasional cutting of corners might save you a second, but do this all the time and you lose performance.
- Likewise, stay off grass and grit. Grass offers no grip whatsoever. It may be tempting to mount the grit traps when overtaking, but they slow you down so much that you're likely to slip down the rankings.
- Don't make sharp turns while accelerating, or hit the accelerator while cornering. This is a sure-fire way to spin the car.

THE TRACKS
Australia: Albert Park

This track starts with a long straightaway, so build up speed and get a good start. There's an easy right then left sequence of corners, followed by a long straight where you have the chance to make up some places. Now you must navigate a sharp right/left chicane, so watch yourself. There's another long straightaway followed by this sequence: right, left, right, a short straight section, right, left. After another short straight is the second chicane and two hard right-hand turns—the pit lane is on your right. Finally, make the last right turn, back onto the starting straightaway.

Brazil: Interlagos

The first straightaway is long and the track is wide—you should
be able to climb a few places off the grid. The first three bends
are shallow and hardly slow you at all, then there's another
straight section, this time ending in a very tight bend. Another
straight and a medium right later, you hit a fairly rapid left/right
combination, followed by a very tight corner—take extreme
care. A series of fast lefts leads you into the grid, and you have
finished the lap.

Argentina: Buenos Aires

The first two turns are lefts, and neither present too great a
problem. The third bend, a right, is not too sharp but its length
can be deceptive. There are two more just like it, so get ready.

A reasonable straight section leads into a couple of medium
rights (this is a good place to overtake), a chicane and two lefts,
though these aren't too tricky. Afterward, however, is a very
sharp left, followed by a series of mid-level turns—be careful
during this section. A medium right and a gentle left later, and
you're back at the starting grid.

Europe: Nurburgring

Another track which starts with a long straightaway then turns
sharply to the right. This is followed by a sharp left and another
straight section, so get yourself onto the racing line on the bends
and prepare for a passing opportunity. Two milder bends later,
you're on another straight section. You should be making
progress by now. There's a long right at the first time extension
and a quick left/right straight after. A right corner followed by a
left takes you to a long straightaway, interrupted only by a gentle
right turn. There are two quick bends then another right leading
to the end of the lap.

San Marino: Imola

Imola is cursed by its narrow
track, so overtaking is
difficult. Move up the ranks
as soon as you begin—it's a
while before you hit the first
curve, a left. Soon after
you're flung into a deceptive
right—don't drift too wide.

Straight sections separate each of a series of lefts, then two rights and a very gentle left drift lead to another straight. This is the place to overtake, but watch out for the chicane at the end. A very fast section follows, interrupted only by shallow drifts. This leads into a 90° left, followed by another almost as sharp. A second section containing only gentle bends ends in a chicane, then hit the pedal until you reach the line.

Monaco: Monte Carlo

This one's full of narrow track and tight turns. A good qualifying time is essential. Take every opportunity to overtake, and guard your position jealously. Keep away from the walls, too—one mistake and you're finished. There's a tight turn near the start, so don't accelerate too quickly. A series of bends follows, offering little in the way of passing opportunities. Watch out for the sharp right as the course veers away from the straight but the road carries on—this can be extremely confusing, so watch the road. Next is a double turn where the track widens slightly. If you're ready to overtake, this is a good place. Next is a gentle turn under a tunnel—again, overtake here. Now it's more tight, narrow turns as the race slows down into the final section of the track.

Spain: Catalunya

This course starts with a long straightaway, so immediately climb through the race order. At the end is a sharp right, followed by another right; although longer, you can take this one faster. Next is a similar right, but the following left needs to be taken slower. After a short straight section, a left drift is followed by a sharp left—don't try to accelerate around this. Then there's a similar drift and bend, this time to the right, ending in a long straight section. A series of sweeping turns, mainly right, lead to another straightaway. This takes you back to the start.

Canada: Montreal

The first two bends are shallow, but the narrow track makes overtaking difficult while the cars are bunched together. Climb a few places as you take the long, gentle right and the sharper (but still straightforward) left that follows. The next few bends are simple drifts, taking you through the first time extension and into a long straightaway. A simple chicane later and you're into another straight section, ending in a leftward drift. Next is the

sharpest bend yet, a 90° right, so take care on approach. On the following straight watch out for the red and white track markings—this is a nasty chicane, so check your speed. A few gentle drifts later, you come against a double swerve—approach too fast and you're on the grass. Then speed past the cranes and hit the finish line.

France: Mangy-Cours

A short straightaway ends in a tough left—make sure you don't overshoot. The proceeding mild chicane leads to a gentle but long right. At the end of the straight section is a tight right—slow down. A further straightaway ends in a chicane, followed by a medium bend. Two tight turns lead to a long right, then another chicane and turn. You're then on the opening straightaway—pick up speed and cross the line.

Great Britain: Silverstone

Here you actually start on a turn, although luckily it's a very gentle right. Pick up a few places from the start before the cars slide into the racing line for the first corner, a right. As you settle into the straight section, jockey for position—this course allows a lot of overtaking. The chicane at the end of the straight isn't too taxing, nor are the two swerving bends immediately after it. There's a long straightaway that's ideal for overtaking, but don't miss the hard right at the end of it. Don't try to cut it by throwing your car over the grit, either—you lose too much speed. A sharp left follows, then a long right, so get on the racing line. There's a chicane and a corner disguised by the fact that the track also continues. Watch out for this. The final section is the slowest part of the circuit and consists of very long turns. Hold the racing line and guard your position, hopefully gaining ground on the guy ahead of you. Don't try to overtake yet—wait until after you have crossed the line and started your next lap.

Germany: Hockenheim

Another course with more straight sections than corners, this is where the slower teams really struggle. Pick your position as you

go into the first right bend and you should come out of it extremely quickly, gaining places as you go. There's an extremely long straightaway next, ideal for taking the weaker cars or back-markers. You can afford to clip the road edge on the chicane, but don't go too far into it. Another long straight section ends in a triple turn—take the racing line or you lose time. Next is a long right and an even longer straightaway. The triple turn at the end barely slows you down. After another long straight section, make a right. Don't run too wide and onto the grass. The track winds a little here, the slowest part of the course, before you get to the starting line.

Hungary: Hungaroring

The first bend is a medium right that proves tricky when the racers are bunched together. A long, hard left slows the race down. A right turn later and you're on the straight again, but next the track twists and turns. Watch the road edge to anticipate the whereabouts and ferocity of corners. Keep the racing line for the awkward chicane, then prepare for a left turn. Three corners of varying speeds follow, the last being the harshest, then a solid right/slight left combination as you go through the time extension. A long left leads into an equally hard right, then you have finished the lap.

Belgium: Spa-Francorchamps

There's an incredibly tight turn as soon as you begin. You could lose several race positions by sliding off into the barriers. An almost straight section follows, with only very gentle drifts. After this is a triple turn chicane, but it's not too tricky. Don't be caught out by the long right or sharp left which follow. A long straight section is followed by a long left, though it's not too sharp; keep the racing line and rocket around it. Now the track turns right twice—take these corners at speed. Subsequent turns are little more than drifts, but this ends with a small semi-circular island. Go left around this—try to cut it out and you come to grief against a barrier. After that, it's plain sailing to the line.

Italy: Monza

At the end of the straightaway you're thrown into a chicane. Make sure you don't get squeezed by other cars as you enter. After a long right drift, you hit another chicane. This one is easier because by now the cars have spread out. A couple of long rights and you cross a series of turns. The right-hander leading to the pit lane is so gentle you can charge through, overtaking anyone who decides to go in the pits, then it's a straight ride to the line.

Portugal: Estoril

This course starts with a very long straightaway, but prepare for the sharp right that follows it or you won't make it around. This is followed by right turns of varying sharpness, then a medium left gives way to a gentle right. A sweeping left is a great opportunity to force your way through on the inside and overtake. Next are two rights then a left. Again, you can squeeze up a place or two by leaving the racing line, but don't cut in front of another car and get a shunt up the rear. Take a long right and hit the pedal for the straightaway. This takes you to the end of the lap.

Japan: Suzuka

At the start there's a punishing right hairpin. Don't jockey for position too soon or you're forced onto the gravel. The next turn is gentle, but the track is narrow—not ideal overtaking territory. A long straight ends in two rights. The track swerves left then right in a gentle chicane. Make sure you take the racing line, as explained earlier. A few bends later you hit a series of tight corners. After a long drift to the right comes an equally long but sharper left. A few tight corners later and you're back to the starting line.

CHEATS

Bonus Car

When you finally become World Grand Prix Champion, turn on the N64 and hold **A+B** when the screen says, "Now loading the data from controller pak..." Now go to the Driver Selection screen and the '96 Forti drivers now have the Ubi Soft Original H-RA V12 car!

Unlimited Fuel

Before you begin any Grand Prix race, set your fuel to just 10%—the reduced weight allows maximum acceleration. Don't worry, you won't lose any fuel during the race!

FIFA: ROAD TO WORLD CUP '98
BASIC SOCCER SKILLS

Manual Goalkeepers
Controlling your own goalkeeper is a difficult business and is therefore only recommended to expert players. Once you have had plenty of practice at using the out-field players and feel comfortable with the sport, you can think about controlling the keeper.

When you have a manual goalkeeper, you become responsible for him when the ball comes within range. The most important thing to remember is not to dive too early, as this gives the advancing attacker more goal to aim at. Stand up and make him go for his shot first.

Tackling

The key to successful tackling is to be hard but fair—basically this means get the ball, not the guy you're tackling! If you're too heavy-handed, you be penalized and find yourself losing players before you even reach half-time!

The best way to tackle an opponent is to approach him from the front or side, then delay the challenge till the last possible moment. This way you should avoid the early tackles that almost always result in a foul move.

Substitutions

In long matches, you need to make substitutions, and this requires a little more than simply bringing on the first player on the subs list! If you're leading a match and want to hold out for a win, take off a tired striker and bring on a defender to help prevent the opposition scoring. This works in reverse: If you're losing and need a goal, take off a defender, replace him with a striker, and go for glory!

GOALS GALORE!

The most important skill in football is undoubtedly scoring—without it, even the most skilled passing and defending won't get you far. This section helps you improve your ability to score goals using the major attacking methods. You should then be able to make the most of any chances that come your way by at least forcing the goalkeeper to make a save.

Penalty Area

In real soccer, most goals are scored from around this region, but surprisingly it's one of the hardest places to score from in *FIFA: Road to World Cup '98*. The advantage lies with the goalkeeper in this situation. The attacking player must have a combination of skill, accuracy, and power (plus a little bit of luck) in order to beat the keeper. Try and wait for your striker to make a run toward the penalty area, then get the ball to him and let him do what he does best—put the ball in the back of the net. Check out the following to see what we mean:

From midfield, use the **B** button to "pass" the ball into the 25-yard area (the actual Pass button—**A**—isn't powerful enough so the ball may be intercepted) and get your striker ready to receive it. As soon as he gets possession of the ball, hold down the **B** button and begin to charge-up a powerful shot.

The most important thing to remember when shooting from this close to the goal is that you should keep the shot low down—if you kick it high, it will be easily saved by the goalkeeper. Let go of the **B** button and immediately hold the joystick in either the bottom-right or bottom-left corner. The only thing that can stop this sort of shot hitting the back of the net is a piece of magic from the keeper.

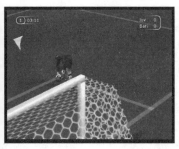

Long Shots

At long range, the most important factor is how hard the player can kick the ball. Basically, how high is his shot power? Remember that it doesn't have to be a striker: Some of the most powerful kicking boots in the game of soccer belong to midfield and even defensive players.

The biggest problem you come up against when trying to

give a defender a few shots at goal is getting him within range. Not only does it leave you a man short at the back, but he may be tackled on his way up the field and give the opposition a chance to break. However, his shot power around the goal should more than make up for this defensive worry. Choosing a good attacking formation is a must, as it pushes your players forward, meaning he has less ground to cover.

Free Kicks

Taking free kicks in *FIFA* is a tricky business. It requires a good touch when you aim the yellow arrow that affects the direction of the kick, and the right skills from the man taking the free kick. You can select which player will take free kicks, so do this before the match begins—it's useless having a guy with poor shot accuracy and power taking your set pieces.

As with shots taken from the penalty area, you must keep free kicks as low as possible and aim to the left or right side of the goal—aiming them straight at the goalkeeper makes his job much easier. Hold down the **B** button for at least five seconds to develop plenty of power, then hold the joypad in one of the bottom corners.

Overhead Kicks

The most elaborate goal in the game, the overhead kick is extremely difficult. It requires good shot accuracy and power to get the ball in the net. You can score one of these "wonder goals" in one of two ways. Firstly, you can flick the ball into the air and use a bicycle kick to aim it toward the goal with the same player. This way is as hard as it sounds, requiring a good touch and excellent ball control.

The second method is to cross the ball in from the side of the pitch then meet it in the penalty area with the guy you want to do the overhead shot. This method doesn't require a particularly good ball control rating, but a high awareness percentage is essential.

The second type of overhead kick is recommended if you have the chance to set up the cross and make the pass, as it has a higher success rating. If you're on a solo break, the one-man overhead can still work, but it's much harder.

CHEATS

Tiny Players

Choose "Player Edit," select Vancouver from the United States League, then enter **KERRY** as a player name. When the men get on the pitch, they're all the size of children's league players!

Invisible Players

Choose "Player Edit," select Sheffield Wednesday from the English League, then enter **WAYNE** as the player name. Your players will be invisible on the pitch!

No Stadium

If you love wide, open spaces, choose "Player Edit," select any team, then input the player's name as **CATCH22**. When the match starts, the soccer stadium won't be there!

Pen and Ink Mode

For an unusual graphic style, choose "Player Edit," select Canada from CONCACAF, and use **MARC** as a player name.

GOLDENEYE 007
WEAPONS TACTICS

- In some games, you can plod through levels with little regard for what weapon you've equipped. *GoldenEye* has a weapons roster comparable to its intricate gameplay. Using your "favorite" weapon, instead of the "appropriate" weapon will usually purchase you a body bag. The key to success can be as simple as using the right tool for the job—if you're in a wide open area and have a Sniper Rifle, target your opponent with the cross hairs (the **L** button), zoom in (the up '**C**' button), and pick them off from out of their range!

- Perhaps the game's most important weapons tactic is to use your weapon's reticle to target a foe's head. A shot here is lethal and drops an enemy quickly, allowing you to conserve precious ammo. It's well worth the time it takes to practice your marksmanship. As you progress deeper into the game, the ability to make quick, precise shots often means the difference between success and failure.

- For those who can't shoot with pinpoint accuracy, it generally takes two shots to the chest region, or five shots to the arms and/or legs, to finish off an opponent. You'll also find that some of your opponents wear helmets—adjust your aim accordingly. And don't let up, no matter how wildly your foe gesticulates, until he drops his weapon. This is the only sure sign that he no longer poses a threat.

- When you fire an automatic weapon, holding the Fire button down disperses your bullets as rapid fire. However, if your ammo clip runs out, you can't reload until you take your finger off the Fire button. In the heat of battle, every second counts, so don't be caught short.

- Remember that it's possible to reload a weapon that's not yet empty. Say you're in a safe area and have one shot left in your gun. When you run into trouble, you'll get only one shot off before you must stop to reload. Refresh your ammo clip every time it's safe to do so, however, and you'll enjoy a noticable difference in your gunplay.

- Check each door to see if it has a window. Rather than barge through into a massacre, stand at the doorway and snipe soldiers through the window. Then prepare to defend yourself as the remaining soldiers converge.

Double Fisting

Throughout the game you'll notice certain enemies toting two guns. If you're in the mood for some double-barreled action, execute one of these enemies and collect their weapons—start looking around when you reach Section Two: The Bunker. Now you can deliver double damage!

SURVIVAL TACTICS

- *GoldenEye* isn't your standard 3-D shooter. You can't rush through the levels blasting away as you might in, say, *Quake* or *Duke Nukem*, for example. Stealth is crucial here, so unless you're in a level with a time limit, take your time and make every shot count.

- Avoiding being shot at by multiple people may seem obvious, but every time you get hit you'll lose control of your character momentarily—and in a firefight, you haven't a moment to lose!

- There are no health power-ups in *GoldenEye*. Every hit you take jeopardizes your ability to complete a level successfully. Exercise caution at all times. It really is better to be safe than sorry.

- Using Lean and Duck maneuvers in gun battles makes you a more elusive target. Leaning allows you to pop out from behind cover to take a clean shot, exposing only a portion of your body to danger. Alternatively, you move just around the corner, shoot until your clip is running low, and lean back out of the line of fire to reload—your opponents don't seem to target your legs very efficiently. Finally, try shooting from a crouch. You'll offer a much smaller target.

- Another important tactic is the Sidestep. Often, an enemy waits to blast you when you walk past a corner. If you walk into this exposed position with your side to the open corner, you're likely to get hit as you turn toward the enemy. But if you stop walking before the corner, turn toward it, and Sidestep out, you'll be ready to fire.

- When taking cover, avoid hiding behind destructible objects. If you're nearby when enemy fire destroys them, you'll take serious damage—and possibly lose your life.

- Learn to hide around solid corners when a pack of soldiers is after you. Turn and wait for them as they approach. Then, as each pops around the corner, give them a head shot or two and wait for the next guy.

CHEATS

GoldenEye contains a number of hidden cheat options. To enable the various cheats on the Cheat Menu, perform the following:

Paintball Mode
In Mission One, Section One, complete the level in Secret Agent Mode in under 2 minutes 40 seconds.

Invincibility
In Mission One, Section Two, complete the level in 00 Agent Mode in under 2 minutes 5 seconds.

DK Mode
In Mission One, Section Three, complete the level in Agent Mode in under 5 minutes.

2 x Grenade Launcher
In Mission Two, Section One, complete the level in Secret Agent Mode in under 3 minutes 30 seconds.

2 x Rocket Launcher
In Mission Two, Section Two, complete the level in 00 Agent Mode in under 4 minutes.

Turbo Mode
In Mission Three, Section One, complete the level in Agent Mode in under 3 minutes.

No Radar Mode
In Mission Four, Section One, complete the level in Secret Agent Mode in under 4 minutes 30 seconds.

Tiny Bond Mode
In Mission Five, Section One, complete the level in 00 Agent Mode in under 4 minutes 15 seconds.

2 x Throwing Knives
In Mission Five, Section Two, complete the level in Agent Mode in under 1 minute 30 seconds.

Fast Animation Mode
In Mission Six, Section One, complete the level in Secret Agent Mode in under 3 minutes and 15 seconds.

Invisibility Mode
In Mission Six, Section Two, complete the level in 00 Agent Mode in under 1 minute 20 seconds.

Enemy Rockets
In Mission Six, Section Three, complete the level in Agent Mode in under 1 minute 45 seconds.

Slow Animation Mode
In Mission Six, Section Four, complete the level in Secret Agent Mode in under 1 minute 30 seconds.

Silver PP7
In Mission Six, Section Five, complete the level in 00 Agent Mode in under 5 minutes 25 seconds.

2 x Hunting Knives
In Mission Seven, Section One, complete the level in Agent Mode in under 3 minutes 45 seconds.

Infinite Ammo Mode
In Mission Seven, Section Two, complete the level in Secret Agent Mode in under 10 minutes.

2 x RC-P90s
In Mission Seven, Section Three, complete the level in 00 Agent Mode in under 9 minutes 30 seconds.

Gold PP7
In Mission Seven, Section Four, complete the level in Agent Mode in under 2 minutes 15 seconds.

Cougar Magnum
In Mission Seven, Section Four, complete the level in Agent Mode

in over 2 minutes 15 seconds.

2 x Lasers
In Mission Eight, Section One, complete the level in Secret Agent Mode in under 9 minutes.

All Guns
In Mission Nine, Section One, complete the level in 00 Agent Mode in under 6 minutes.

Golden Gun
In Mission Nine, Section One, complete the level in 00 Agent Mode in over 6 minutes.

007 Mode
Completing Missions One through Nine in 00 Agent Mode, allows you access to a level editor option, where you can alter game variables.

Hidden Levels
● To play Aztec Complex (Mission Eight, Section One), complete the game in Secret Agent Mode.
● To play Egyptian Temple (Mission Nine, Section One), complete the game in 00 Agent Mode.

LAMBORGHINI CHALLENGE
GAME BASICS

● The cars are very responsive and it's possible to take many of the corners at full speed, even when it seems impossible to do so! Use the first lap of the race to test out the corners of the track, so you know which ones you can take at full speed and which ones you have to slow down for. This means that your first lap may not be a scorcher, but subsequent ones will benefit from the knowledge you have gained.

● Whenever you have to make a jump, try and keep the car as

straight as possible just before you take off. If you try and turn the car before you leave the ground, you land side-on and may skid into a wall. It doesn't matter how fast you go, as long as you're not turning when you take off!

● At the start, don't worry if all the computer-controlled cars race past you—no matter how much you try, getting a good start is almost impossible. Concentrate on building up your speed and shifting through the gears before you have to make the first turn. As the race progresses, you'll have plenty of chances to make up places as the CPU vehicles are often slower than yours.

CHEATS AND CODES

Easy Level Codes
Arcade: Basic Series: Porsche 959
Arcade: Pro Series: Ferrari 512 TR
Normal Championship Series: Bugatti EB110 GT

Expert Level Codes
Arcade: Basic Series: Ferrari F-50
Arcade: Pro Series: Dodge Viper GTS
Normal Championship Series: McLaren F1
(reverse tracks are opened)

Reverse Tracks
To race on reversed tracks, beat Championship Mode on Novice and Expert difficulty levels.

MACE: THE DARK AGE
SPECIAL MOVES

Button	Movement	Abbreviations
A	Quick Punch	Q
C(L)	Strong Punch	S
C(U)	Kick	K
Z trigger	Evade	Z
D-pad	Moves Character	D, U, L, R

THE EXECUTIONER

Axe Poke	B+Q
Green Fireball	D, F+Q
Down Power Chop	Q+S
High Chop	B, S
Attack and Throw	B, D, F+S
High-Low Hit	B, F+Q
Axe Sweep, Overhead	D, B+S
Execution	B, D, F, B, D, F+Q (close)

Combo Attacks

Three-hit	Q, Q, S
Three-hit	S, K, Q
Five-hit	B+Q, Q, Q, S, B, D, F+S
Eight-hit	B+Q, Q, Q,S, B, F+Q, D, B+S

LORD DIEMOS

Face Blow	B+Q

Reflect Attack	F, D, B+Q
Bomb Attack	B, D, F+Q
Big Hit	Q+S
Stab then Throw	B+Q+S, then tap Q
Shoulder Attack	F, F+S
Quick Sword Strike	B, F+S
Kick Low	B, F+K
Execution	F, B, D, F+S (half screen)

Combo Attacks

Three-hit	S, D+S, D+S
Three-hit	S, S, Q+S
Six-hit	B+S, S, S, B, D, F+S, F, F+S

RAGNAR

Running Chop	Q+S
Running Head	B+Q+S
Multi Chops	F+Q (tap rapidly)
Lightning Blast	B, F+Q
Axe Smash	Q+S+K
Rolling High	B, F+K
Double High	B, D, F+S
Fake Roll	F, F+K
Execution	B, D, F, B+K (close)

Combo Attacks

Two-hit	Q+S+K, S (juggle combo)
Three-hit	S, Q, Q
Three-hit	Q, S, Q+S
Five-hit	S, Q, Q, B, F+K

KOYASHA

Double Backflip	B+Z
Lunging Knife	Q+S
Fire Blast	D, F+Q
Double Fire Blast	D, F+Q,Q
Rolling Slash	Z+S
Leg Cutter	F, D, B+S
Slide Kick	B, F+K
Downward Kick	F, D, B+K
Leaping Kicks	D, F+K
Air Flip Throw	UF+Q+S
Low Slash and Upper	F, D, F+S
Crossover Kick	S+K, when jumping over

Execution ....B, F, B, F+Q (close)
Combo Attacks
Two-hit ....S, Z+S
Three-hit...S, Q, K
Four-hit...Q, K, K

TARIA

Dagger Stab...B+Q
Twister..F, D+Q
Fire Blast ....D, F+Q
Air Fireball..jump, then D, F+Q
Spinning Low Slices ....F, D, B+S
Running Slash ....B, F+S
Reaching Slash....................................Q+S
Low Reaching Slash ....S+K
Flash Kick...D, F+K
Execution ....hold S, then release (one step)
Combo Attacks
Two-hit ....U+K, D, F+K
Three-hit...UF+K, K, D, F+K
Three-hit...S, K, K
Three-hit...Q, Q, S
Five-hit...B+Q, Q, Q, S, D, F+K
Seven-hit...B+Q, S, K, K, F, D, B+S, D, F+K

AL' RASHID

Flashcut ....D, F+S
Flashcut follow-up..............................after Flashcut, D, F+Q
Air Dive..jump, then B, F+Q
Sand Devil...hold S, then release
Double Chop ....Q+S
Sword Upper ....F, D, F+S
Block and Chop ....B+S
Tornado..F, D, B+S
Side Kick ....B, F+K
Side Kick Follow-up ....after Side Kick, F+S
Execution ....B, D, F, B+S (third screen)
Combo Attacks
Three-hit...K, Q, K
Three-hit...S, S, Q

TAKESHI

Sword Flurry ....F+Q (rapidly)
Flame Slash ....D, B+S
Uppercut Slash ....B, D, F+S
Sword Sweep ....D+Q+S
Energy Ball ....B, F+S, then S
Side Kick ....B, F+K
High Sword ....Q+S
Low Sword ....S+K
Execution ....F, D, B, D, F+S (close)

Combo Attacks
Three-hit ....Q, Q, S
Three-hit ....S, Q, S
Three-hit ....B, F+S, S, B, D, F+S
Four-hit ....D, B+S, Q, Q, B, D, F+S
Six-hit ....D, B+S, Q, Q, S, B, F+S, S

NAMIRA

Special Moves
Double High Slash ....B, Q, Q
Double Low Slash ....B, S, S
Sword Slash ....Q+S
Sword Sweep ....S+K
Sword Spin ....Q+S+K
Splits Kick ....B, F+K
Chop Kick ....D, F+K
Punt Kick ....F, F+K
Fireball ....F, B+Q
Execution ....D, D, B, F, K (close)

Combo Attacks

Three-hit .... K, Q, S
Three-hit .... K, K, B+K
Three-hit .... U+K, B, Q, Q
Four-hit .... jump+K, K, K, F, F+K
Five-hit .... B, S, S, B, Q, Q, F, F+K

XIAO LONG

Double Backflip .... B+Z
Low Staff Hit .... B, Q
Staff Sweep .... D, F+Q
Spinning Smash .... Q+S
Stomp Combo .... F, D, B+S
Staff Uppercut .... B, D, F+S
Staff Combo .... hold S for three seconds
Flying Kick .... B, D, F+K
Block and Kick .... F, D, B+K
Advancing Strike .... B, F+Q
Crossover .... Kick while jumping over, S+K
Execution .... B, F, B, F+S (close)

Combo Attacks

Three-hit .... Q, K, K
Three-hit .... S, Q, K
Four-hit .... hold S, U+K, S
Six-hit .... jump+K, Q, K, K, F, D, B+S

MORDOS KULL

Block and Low Swing .... F, D, B+Q
Stunning Mace .... Q+S
Power Swing .... B+Q+S
Double Mace Swing .... B, D, F+S
Shield Blast .... B, F+S
Block and High Swing .... F, D, B+S
Uppercut Swing .... F, D, F+S
Side Kick Combo .... B, F+K, repeat twice
Execution .... D, D, B+S (close)

Combo Attacks

Three-hit .... Q, S, Q
Three-hit .... S, Q, B+S
Four-hit .... K, B, F+K, B, F+K, B, F+K
Eight-hit .... Q, S, Q, B, D, F+S, B, F+K, B, F+K, B, F+K

DREGAN

Block and Low Strike	F, D, B+Q
Evil Strike	Q+S
Skull Ball	D, F+Q
Spin Kicks	hold S for three seconds
Block and High Strike	F, D, B+S
Sword Uppercut	F, D, F+S
Body Lunge	B, F+S
Low Kick	B, D, F+K
Leg Drop	B, F+K
Kick and Pounce	S+K
Execution	F, D, B, D, F+K (close)

Combo Attacks

Three-hit	Q, Q, S
Three-hit	S, S, Q

HELL KNIGHT

Double Chop	B+Q+S
Flame Columns	B, F+Q
Big Upper	Q+S
Block and Low Strike	F, D, B+Q
Tail Blast	D, F+Q
Tail Strike Combo	D, F+S
Block and High Strike	F, D, B+S
Double Axe Ram	B, F+S
Axe Grab	B, D, F+S
Kick Down	B, F+K
Execution	B, D, F, B+K

Combo Attacks

Three-hit	S, S, Q
Three-hit	K, S, S
Six-hit	S, S, Q, D, F+S, S, D, F+Q

POJO

Egg Launch	jump, then Q+S
Jumping Back Attack	F, D, B+S
Running Charge	B, F+Q
Flying Scratch	B, F+K
Atomic Blast	Q+S+K
Execution	hold F+K (close)

Combo Attacks

Two-hit	K, K

Three-hit...Q, Q, S
Three-hit...S, S, Q

GRENDAL

Elbow Smash ....B, F+Q
Running Attack ....B+Q+S
Knockdown ....Q+S
Uppercut Smash.................................B, F+S
Triple Overhead ....F+Q+S, Q+S, Q+S
Fist Sweep..F, D, B+S
Shoulder Ram ....F, F+S
Power Stomp ....Q+S+K
Knee...B+K
Execution ....D, D, B , F+K (close)
Combo Attacks
Five-hit...B+K, K, F+Q+S, Q+S, Q+S
Seven-hit...B+S, S, B, F+Q, Q, F+Q+S, Q+S, Q+S

WAR MECH

Uppercut Mace...................................B, F+Q
Spinning Mace ....Q+S
Ground Pound ....F, D+Q
Low Cannonball ....D, F+Q
Mid Cannonball ....D, F+S
Arm Poke...B, F+S
Triple Swing.......................................hold S for three seconds
Hyper Hammer ....F+S (tap rapidly)
Flip Kick ....B, D, F+K
Stomp ....Q+S+K
Execution ....B, F, D, B+S (close)
Combo Attacks
Five-hit...Q, Q, S
Five-hit...S, S, Q+S

ICHIRO

Shove ....F, F+Q
Fireball ....D, F+Q
Spinning Double Slash......................B, F+Q
Slash Combo......................................B, Q, S
Sword Sweep ....F, D, B+Q
Sword Thrust ....Q+S
Leaping Slash ....B, S

Flame Jump	B, D, F+S
Low Slash	F, D, B+S
Gut Punch Combo	B, F+S, then quick repeat twice
Sword Sweep	D+Q+S
Flash Kick	B, D, F+K
Power Slash	S+K
Execution	F, D, B, D, F+S (close)

Combo Attacks

Three-hit	S, S, Q
Three-hit	Q, S, K
Three-hit	S+K, S, Q
Four-hit	F, F+Q, S, S, D, F+Q
Seven-hit	B, S, S, S, Q, B, Q, S, B, D, F+S

CHEATS

Play as Pojo!

After performing Taria's Execution, where she turns her victim into a chicken, start a two-player game and highlight Taria. Hold the **Start** button while pressing **A** or **B**. Release **Start** when the first round begins.

Play as Grendal

Get three wins in one-player mode and start a two-player game. Highlight the Executioner and hold **Start** while pressing **A** or **B**. Hold **Start** until the fight begins.

Play as Ichiro and Warmech

Reset the Nintendo 64. During the legal screen, perform these movements on the joypad: **Right, Up, Left, Down, Right, Up, Left, Down** (basically a counterclockwise circle, twice). You should hear a sound that indicates the cheat has worked. Warmech and Ichiro are located above the Executioner and Lord Diemos on the selection screen.

Unlimited Credits

When you get KO'ed in a one-player game, quickly press the Start button on the other controller. Now when this match has finished, you can fight the computer again. This can be done as many times as you wish.

Change Colors

To change your fighter's color, press and hold any of the **C** buttons while the desired fighter is selected. To confirm your selection, press the **Z** trigger button, then **A** to begin the game.

Fighters with Bunny Slippers

At the character select screen, move the cursor to the following fighters and press the **Start** button on each: Ragnar, Dregan, Koyasha. Now simply choose your fighter and press **A** to begin the fight.

Level Select

To select a particular stage in which to fight, go to the relevant character's portrait on the player select screen and tap the **Start** button four times. Select your character as normal.

Screen Adjustment

To adjust the screen, hold the **L+R+Z** buttons and move the analog pad and joypad in the same direction.

Secret Battles

To unlock each secret battle, move to each character listed and tap Start after each one. Go to your desired character and select as usual. All of these secrets are for two-player mode, except for the "Random AI" cheat, which is for a one-player game.

Battle Characters

Lava Castle	Mordos Kull, Taria, Ragnar
Big Heads	Ragnar, Al' Rashid, Takeshi
Random AI	Hell Knight, Xiao Long, Dregan, Namira
Gold Stage	Koyasha, Mordos Kull, Takeshi

Small Fighters

At the character selection screen, highlight Takeshi and press **Start**. Now highlight Al' Rashid and press **Start** again. Repeat this pattern with Ragnar and Xiao Long, then select your character as normal.

Switch Heads

At the character select screen, move the cursor to the following fighters and press **Start** on each one: Al' Rashid, Takeshi, Mordos

Kull, Xiao Long, and Namira. Now simply choose your fighter and press the **A** button.

Two-Player Practice Mode
To use the two-player practice mode, highlight the Practice option and hit the Start button on both controllers simultaneously. Now both players can select a character as normal, but when the battle starts there are no life bars! The fight can last forever!

MADDEN 64
GENERAL TIPS

- Try and vary your plays as much as possible. Use a couple of running plays, as this brings the defensemen forward, in anticipation of another run, leaving the secondary open and the wide receivers poorly covered. Usually, you can then gain good yardage with little trouble. Mixing your play selection is crucial, especially when up against teams with a good defense, as they pick up on your tactics very quickly.
- Near the end of the half or game, try and run the clock down as much as you can. Manipulating the clock is a sneaky way of putting pressure on the opposing team's offense: If you can waste a couple of minutes while driving downfield, then score, they have a bigger deficit to pull back and less time to do it in. The best plays for doing this are running plays. Always be sure you're tackled in bounds, as running out of bounds stops the clock.
- Use trick play occasionally, as it serves to unsettle the opposing defense. The "Draw" and "Play Action" plays are good examples of this and make it extremely difficult for the defensive linemen and backfield markers to work out where the ball is going.
- If you're losing, try to avoid calling a running play in the final stage of a game. The fourth quarter is make or break, the time to come up with some big plays. You should be looking up top for the big yardage makers or that clock will have run down before you know it!

- Try not to waste time-outs in the early stages of a half. You only get three, which ideally should be saved until the last few minutes. Using your time-outs correctly can save you the game in the dying seconds of a close match.

- Do not take unnecessary risks in the early stages of a game. If you get down to your opponent's red zone then find you can't progress the ball any further, take the easy field goal. At this stage, it's more important to get three points on the board rather than try for six but fail.

- Do not waste possession of the ball. If you can score on every drive, you put great pressure on the opponent's offense to come up with big plays when they get the ball.

CHEATS

Bonus Teams

To access these bonus teams, do the following: Go into Season mode, then select the "Create a player" option. Input his name as one of the codes below, then save the information. Now select Exhibition mode and the corresponding team will be available.

Code	Team
TIBURON	All Madden
SIXTIES	1960s team
SEVENTIES	1970s team
EIGHTIES	1980s team
HOWLIE AFC	Pro Bowl 1996?97

View Ending Sequences

To see some of the cool real-time rendered winning sequences, turn on your N64 and hold the **L shoulder, R shoulder,** and **Z** buttons when the EA logo appears.

Random Team Select

Go to the "Select team" menu in Exhibition mode and press, **C(U)** and **C(R)** at the same time.

MISCHIEF MAKERS
CHEATS

Air Boost

You can gain extra altitude with the Air Boost. While jumping, press the joypad twice in the desired direction, or just the appropriate **C** button.

Ball Hop

The balls that sit in mid-air—basically small, round Clancers—can easily be jumped between. Move to the left or right and hold **Up** or **Down** to aim yourself at the next ball, press **B** to jump, then **B** again to grab.

Springing

Balls on springs can be used to gain altitude. Grab onto it and Air Boost to compress the spring; release to be launched through the air. Some springs can be aimed, too.

Shaking

You can make progress by pressing **Down** twice or **C(D)** to shake a ball. This can extend its range or rotate it. Shaking a jar mixes its contents. Six blue gems make a green gem, two green gems give a yellow gem, mix two flowers to create a throwing star, three throwing stars for a boomerang, and four grenades/mines can be shaken up to make a bomb. When holding the jar, press **Down** to see inside and **Left and Right shoulder** buttons to pick an item. Shaking a weapon can increase its power.

Yellow Gems

To get the best ending to the game, you need to find all 52 yellow gems. There's one hidden in every level. In the case of boss levels, gems are earned by performed spotlessly, rather than found. The more gems you get, the more of the end sequence is displayed. The ending also depends on how quickly you completed the levels—you should aim for "A" ratings.

MORTAL KOMBAT MYTHOLOGIES: SUB-ZERO
THE FINAL BOSSES

In the Fortress you must defeat three female guardians in order to get the crystals that power the teleporter and give access to Quan Chi's lair. Here's how to defeat the guardians and their masters.

Kia

She doesn't look like an assassin, but Kia's certainly fast. She's armed with boomerang blades that can catch you as they're thrown, then again when they whip back toward her. You must dodge the initial attack to stand any chance of beating her. She throws these blades at high and low heights, so ducking won't save you.

Press Block whenever you're not attacking, then use an Ice Blast and Roundhouse Kick combo. If you follow up with a horizontal Ice Blast, you can catch Kia as she gets up.

Make sure your Ice Meter is high before you start and commence your combos from the far side of her lair. The sequence can be repeated for as long as the Ice Meter holds out, taking around one third of her energy.

Kia also uses lots of Sweeps and combinations of Kick attacks. You can Sweep, too, but never use more than two in a row, or she wises up and counterattacks with a Jump Kick.

Jataaka

She's as fast as Kia but more powerful. Block the bolts launched from her sword. When she's winding up for a laser sword attack, use the Ice Blast to counterattack. You may get hit by a laser blast, but you'll also freeze her. You can now use the tactics given for Kia, using Ice Blast and Roundhouse combos to repeatedly knock her across the screen.

Jataaka sometimes dashes toward you with a three-hit sword combo that you must block or take chunks of damage. She's also fond of sweeping Sub-Zero off his feet, so be prepared to leap away.

Sareena

One swipe from Sareena's blades knocks Sub-Zero's energy bar out of the ball park. She's also fond of spinning like a tornado, whipping into Sub-Zero with great ferocity.

Sareena is fractionally faster than her fellow assassins and a more accomplished fighter, unleashing three-Kick and three-Punch combo attacks. You can use the same Ice Blast and Roundhouse Kick tactics to kill Sareena, but change the timing of your Ice Blast. She takes a little longer to get up, so wait a fraction of a second longer. You have the option of performing a Fatality on her. It's wisest to let her live.

Quan Chi
Wait for Quan Chi to run toward you, then rapidly tap the High Punch button. Nine times out of ten, he runs straight into your blows. Follow this up with a horizontal Ice Blast—as he's still reeling from the Punches, he won't block it. Now use the tried and tested Ice Blast and Roundhouse Kick technique.

Continue until you reach the other end of the screen or run out of Ice Energy. Retreat to the opposite side of the screen and wait for him to dash toward you. As he approaches, go for a Low Sweep. Use two Sweeps then Ice Blast him as he's getting to his feet. Return to the Roundhouse Kick and Ice Blast combo.

If Quan Chi traps you in a corner, jump back as far as you can go and use Jump Kicks to knock him to the ground as he walks toward you—he has problems blocking these. His weakest attacks are the three-punch combo and an energy field that draws you toward him: both can be blocked.

He also generates a fireball as he slowly moves across the screen. While he's generating it, use an Ice Blast to freeze him, then even if you don't block the fireball, you can continue attacking with Roundhouse Kicks.

If you didn't use a Fatality on her earlier, Sareena runs onscreen and delivers the killing blow. If you did, use an Uppercut.

Shinnok
Wait for Shinnok's amulet to flash and use the horizontal Ice Blast to freeze him (he can't block while firing). Turn around, run to the far side of the battle area, and use the teleporter.

Now at the opposite side of the arena, quickly fire another Ice Blast. This ensures Shinnok stays frozen long enough for you to do the dirty deed: Dash up to him and press the Use/Action button to grab the amulet, robbing Shinnok of his powers.

Shinnok transforms into a giant beast and tries to pulverize Sub-Zero with his fists. Quickly turn around and run through the portal that has appeared.

PASSWORDS

Having problems finding your way through the maze of water on Level 5, or are the fire pits on Level 6 making things too hot for you? Fear not, here are the passwords for all levels, plus some cheats!

Level 2	THWMSB
Level 3	CMSZDG
Level 4	ZVRKDM
Level 5	JYPPHD
Level 6	RGTKCS
Level 7	QFTLWN
Level 8	XJKNZT
Unlimited Urns	NXCVSZ
1,000 Lives	GTTBHR
View Credits	CRVDTS

Shinnok's Fortress
(press L1 to fight Quan Chi, L2 to fight Shinnok)
....ZCHRRY

FATALITY

You can perform a Fatality on two characters: Scorpion at the end of Level 1, and Sareena on the final stage. The move for both situations is as follows:

Stand close (but not touching), then press **Forward, Down, Forward, High Punch**.

NAGANO WINTER OLYMPICS '98
EVENT TIPS

Downhill Skiing

This is the blue ribbon event of the Winter Olympics, so as you'd expect, it's also one of the toughest. Getting a gold medal here is a real challenge!

However, the controls are quite basic. Simply use the analog joystick to steer your skier as he hurtles down the mountain. Pressing the **A** button increases his turning capability, but also slows him down slightly.

The key to getting a good time in this event is to anticipate the turns of the course so you're always in a good position to ski through gates and make sharp turns. Anticipation of the course means you won't have to use the **A** button to help you make the turns, and this keeps your speed high.

Here's a brief guide to the layout of the downhill course, so you know what to expect: From the start, the course goes straight ahead, then there's an easy right and a long straightaway over a jump, followed by a left. Now you reach a hard right-hand corner, then a hard left, followed by a straight and a sweeping left. Now left again over a jump, then a sweeping left turn into an easy left, followed by an easy right. There's another jump and an easy right before a straight run-in to the finish.

Ski Jump K=90 & K=120

The ski jumping event is split into two different ramp heights, the K=90 and K=120. However, they offer no real difference in gameplay. For example, on the higher ramp you have more wind to contend with, so this makes life a little more difficult.

When the event starts, hold **Down** on the joypad and press the **A** button to send your skier down the ramp. As he reaches the edge, push the pad **Up**, then quickly back to the **Down** position.

Now you must use the joystick to keep your man leaning forward, so his body is approximately 35° to the horizontal. This is where the wind plays a large part in the outcome of your jump—the stronger the wind, the more difficult it is to keep a good position while airborne! As the arrow on the altimeter (located on the far right of the screen) reaches the green area, press the **A** button to perform a landing.

This event seems easy, but it's actually one of the hardest. Keeping a good position in mid-air is difficult and judging the landing is even harder. Practice is the only way to overcome these problems. Start on the smaller K=90 ramp and when you have perfected it, move onto the trickier K=120.

Freestyle Aerials

This event is one of the easiest. Simply choose a trick from the list of ten available, then get onto the slopes and perform it. The more difficult the trick, the more points you're likely to score—provided you pull it off, of course!

This means you should select a trick that's difficult enough to give you good points, but easy enough to perform.

Slowly build up the trick difficulty as you get better at the event, that way you won't attempt too much, too soon. Once you have selected a trick, the view changes to the snow-covered slope and the event automatically starts. As your skier approaches the ramp, repeatedly press the **B** button to gain power. Continue to do this for the entire time he's in the air. Your skier automatically performs your chosen trick. As you attempt your landing, press the **A** button as the skis touch the snow. Remember, a good landing is essential if you want to score top marks.

Snowboard Half-pipe

Here you perform a series of tricks on a snowboard as you slide up and down the sides of the snow-covered half-pipe. You must impress the judges with your stunts to gain the highest possible overall score. Before the event starts, choose eight tricks that you want to perform during your "act."

There are over 20 different tricks in all. The judges are looking for technique, rotation, execution and landing precision, so you need a variety of the difficult and simple to gain a good all-around score.

Once you have selected your tricks, the event begins in

earnest. For each trick, you must perform a series of button presses and joypad moves—the more difficult the trick, the harder the combo of commands. The computer steers your snowboarder through the half-pipe, so all you have to worry about is performing the stunt in time. Fail to complete the button/joypad sequence and your 'boarder performs a basic jump, which won't impress the judges at all!

The key with this event is to avoid going for all hard tricks. It's much better to complete your "act" well and only perform easy tricks than fail to perform harder ones. As you get better at inputting the button commands, you can select more difficult tricks.

Snowboard Giant Slalom

This is essentially the same as the alpine skiing giant slalom. The basic idea is to maneuver your sportsman through a series of gates as you descend the hill. However, the snowboarding version has a much slower pace, and this makes things considerably easier.

The triangular flags that indicate the slalom gates in this event must be passed carefully, as getting too close causes your snowboarder to fall. The red gates must be passed on the left, the blue ones to the right. The gates are pretty much placed in a straight line down the hill; simply weave through them as quickly as possible.

Keeping your speed as high as possible is the key and this means you must use the **A** button as little as possible. This button gives you greater turning ability but slows you down.

Think ahead and try to line your snowboarder up with the next gate as soon as you have passed the previous one. The only thing that can win you this event is old fashioned practice. Get used to steering your player and anticipating the gates and the gold medal will be yours!

Speed Skating 500m & 1500m

This event is quite basic and should pose no problems. The arrow on the power meter (located in the top-right corner of the screen) bounces from side to side

and you must press the **Left** and **Right shoulder** buttons in rhythm with its movements. If you press the buttons out of sequence, your skater loses momentum and slows down; get it right and you gradually increase speed.

The only tricky thing to watch out for is the stamina meter, located directly under the power bar. When this is depleted, your skater stops altogether and you have to wait for his stamina to build up again. This means it's a bad idea to go at full speed at the start of the race. Save some stamina for the final straight to give you a strong finish to the race.

This factor isn't quite as important in the 500 meter event, as this version is basically a sprint. However, in the 1500 meter race, you must pay close attention to your stamina or you may have to stop in mid-race and wait for it to build up.

The Luge

This event has to be one of the maddest sports ever invented! You basically race down a frozen tunnel on a trash can lid! When the event starts, tap the Left and Right shoulder buttons as quickly as possible in order to build up power—the more power you generate, the faster your start. Once you get going, steer your rider through the banked bends, keeping your speed as high as possible. The higher you take the bend, the faster you go, but you run the risk of flipping over. This means disqualification—plus a bad case of ice rash!

The idea is to gain speed safely. Avoid hitting the sides of the luge track, as it reduces speed and also knocks you all over the place, making your "vehicle" much harder to control. To begin with, you'll only be able to achieve average times, but with patience and practice, you'll be up there with the best.

Four-man Bobsled

The bobsled is very similar to the luge, except you control a group of four, as opposed to a single rider. The biggest difference between the two events is at the start. For the bobsled, repeatedly tap the **A** button as quickly as possible to gain speed, but as you do so also push the **B** button, as this tells your riders to jump into the sled.

If you leave this too late, you won't get all four men aboard and you'll be disqualified; if you make them jump in too early, you'll have a slow start. This effectively puts an end to your challenge—no matter how fast you ride the rest of the course, you cannot recover from a poor start!

Practice your timing so you know exactly when to get your team members into the sled. This takes time, so don't expect to get it perfect the first time, but get this part of the event right and you'll be in a good position to achieve a fast time.

Once you have got going, the controls and tactics are the same as the luge: The higher you ride the corner, the faster you go, but you run the risk of crashing. For this reason, adopt the same strategy, concentrating on finishing the race and learning the track. When you know how sharp the corners are and when to turn, you can build up your speed.

Curling

This is probably the best of all the events in Nagano '98 as it requires real skill and tactics, plus it's great fun to play! Curling is basically a game of lawn bowling but played on ice.

Each player has four "stones" which he slides down the rink. The player who gets his stone closest to the center of the target area at the opposite end of the rink wins the round. The winner is the player who has accumulated the most points over four rounds. If a player has more than one stone closest to the target, he scores a point for each.

First select the power and direction of your shot. This is difficult, as it takes experience to work out how much power is required to reach the target area. You can also change the direction in which you spin the stone—effectively, you can "curl" the stone to the right or left.

Once the stone is on its way down the rink, you can use the other two members of your team to "sweep" the ice by rapidly pressing the **A** button. This makes the stone travel slightly further and is useful for gaining more distance, should you need it!

Curling is a game of tactics and skill. You can use stone to block off certain section of the target area and make your opponent's life hell. Take the time to learn how to curl the stone correctly, so you can avoid traps such as this.

The longer you play, the more you'll get the feel for game. Setting the power becomes second nature, then concentrate on using tactics to score points.

Learning when you need to use your team mates to "sweep" the ice is another skill that comes with practice.

Also don't forget that the game is played over four rounds. If you lose the first, don't be discouraged. You can come right back in the second round, planting two stones nearer the bullseye than your opponent and taking the lead.

Giant Slalom

This event isn't as fast as the downhill but requires even greater awareness and anticipation of what lies ahead. You must steer your skier through a series of gates that are set out along the course, and this means that you must always think ahead.

You must line up your skier with the next set of gates, and this requires excellent anticipation. If you fail to pass through a pair of gates, you're automatically disqualified. Once you have lined yourself up to go through the gates you're approaching, you should immediately be thinking about the next set—every second is valuable in the giant slalom!

However, because this event is relatively slow moving and the gates basically alternate left and right, following the course is quite easy. The only thing you must concentrate on is keeping your skier as straight as possible while making the turns safely. Use the **A** button only when it's essential, as doing so lowers your speed.

NBA IN THE ZONE '98
GENERAL TIPS

● Don't commit silly fouls early in a match—you'll pay for them down the stretch! If one of your best players picks up two fouls in the first quarter, you're advised to get them off the court and rest him until at least the second period. Don't forget, on committing the sixth foul, a player must leave the match, and if this means losing your star player at a vital time, you're in trouble! Take it easy in the first half and you can use fouls in the second, when things start heating up.

- A back-court violation is all too easy to commit in the heat of a close game. Don't forget that once an attacking player has advanced the ball over the halfway line, he cannot re-enter his own half. Even if you come up against a double team as you cross into your opponent's half, don't be scared into making the foul. Look for the outlet pass to the free man, as he should be open for the shot.
- Drawing fouls is not easy to do, but it's certainly worth "testing" the defense in the early moments of a game. Give the ball to either of your forwards and let then make a drive to the hoop. If a defending player commits a foul, you're awarded two free throws and the guilty player gets a personal foul! If you do this a couple of times early on in the match you can put some easy points on the board and hopefully put opposing players into early foul trouble!

ON-COURT SKILLS
Shooting

Basically a player can shoot from three areas on the court: inside the paint, inside the three-point circle, and outside the three-point circle. Obviously, it's possible to shoot from further away than the three-point perimeter, but it's not advisable if you want to make the bucket. Shooting from inside the paint is the easiest, simply because it's the closest. Try and give this type of shot to either of your Forwards, or better still, the Center. They are your tallest men and therefore have the best chance of completing the shot—smaller players are usually overpowered by a defender if they shoot from here.

Shooting inside the three-point circle but just outside the painted area is a kind of "no man's land"—it's still close for the small guys, but far enough away to be a problem for your Center. Before shooting, try to get into as much space as possible—if you just have air between your player and the net, you greatly enhance the success rate of your shots. This is where most of the points are earned, so practice shooting from this area.

Remember to pass the ball around and wait for an opening. If you fail to convert a high percentage of shots from this area, you'll be lucky if your team comes out on top. It takes a special kinda guy to shoot from three-point land, but one thing's for certain, the majority of three-point shooters are small and have a good turn of speed. Using a tall player (like the Center) for this type of shot is asking for trouble.

There are a couple of things to remember when attempting this type of shot. First of all, try and get a clear view of the hoop. It's no good having a defender in your face while trying to score from this far out. If need be, pass the ball around and wait for the opening to come.

Secondly, every player has a favorite spot from which to shoot a three-pointer. Finding your three-point shooter's "spot" early in the match is essential if you're to be successful. Don't overuse the three-point shot. The reward is obviously an extra point, but the risk involved means that any team who base their game plan on shooting a high percentage of them is asking to be white-washed. A balanced attack that makes full use of every type of shot is always successful.

Passing

It may seem like the easiest skill in basketball, but fast, accurate passing can be hard to perfect. It's not simply a case of throwing the ball around then shooting when you feel like it. Freeing up your best shooting players for that long jump shot and making plays for your big guys in the paint can all be done through fast passing movements.

The skill that takes the greatest amount of practice is knowing when not to pass the basketball. It may sound stupid, but simply passing the ball around for the sake of it is very dangerous. It gives the opposing team more opportunities to steal the ball, or even make an interception. Be particularly careful of this when playing the ball into the paint, as defenders are better placed to intercept those passes.

When you're on a fast break, passing the basketball becomes very important. It's useless running up the court with the ball after an interception or steal, as by the time you get anywhere near the hoop, the defenders have had a chance to regroup. Make fast, accurate passes without "over passing" and quickly get the ball the player with the best shot at the basket.

Substitutions

When playing in simulation mode, player fatigue is a major factor. As the player runs around the court, they tire, and this is when mistakes start to occur. Common mistakes that tired players make range from little things like bad passes, to more serious errors like fouls. One thing is for sure: the all-important shooting percentage begins to plummet. This makes it essential to

substitute them with a suitable fresh player.

Unless you have absolutely no other choice, the first rule of subbing is never make someone play out of his specialized position. Only a handful of the greatest men in the league can do this; for the majority it spells disaster.

The trick to effective substituting is to keep your team's shape while rotating the personnel on the floor. Change players as often as you can and always try and keep at least one player from the starting line-up on the court at any given time. It's no good using the original five players until each has no energy, then replacing them all with substitutes—you'll get a bunch of rookies on the floor with no one to lead them.

For example, as the starting five begin to tire to about half their original energy, bring on one new Forward and one new Guard. When the remaining three players begin to tire critically, sub three new players in their place, bringing back the two starting guys you took off earlier. This way you always have at least one "go to guy" on the floor in a clutch situation.

The other thing to remember when subbing personnel in and out of a match is always have your best five players on the floor at the end of each half. This is especially critical in the fourth period. It's useless having some freshman taking the match-deciding three-pointer—after all, that's why you have superstars!

At the beginning of each match, you can select your starting five players. This is where a game can be won or lost—putting the wrong player in the wrong position can be a disaster and leave you in trouble before the tip-off has taken place! Below is advice on choosing the best player for each of the five starting positions.

Point Guard

This is your team leader and as such he must be a good all-around player. However, the single most important attribute he must have is ball-handling skill. Every time your team has the ball, this is the guy who's in charge, so it's crucial that he handles the ball well. It's also essential that the Point Guard has a good passing ability to set up the plays.

Shooting Guard

It's fairly obvious that the most important skill rating to look for in this position is shooting ability. However, speed and ball handling skills are equally important. If you can find a player with good ratings in all three areas, make him your starting "two-guard."

Center

When picking a Center, look at his power, height, and blocked shots ratings as a guide to his ability. A good Center must be able to play solid defense and block any shots that are taken within his area. Power and height are also a factor—it's not good having your Center pushed around in the paint. You need someone who will stand tall and strike fear into opposing players.

Power Forward

The Power Forward is the Center's back-up for rebounds and blocking shots, so he must have a strong rating in both categories. He must also have high power, as this gives him the ability to drive to the hoop at the offensive end of the court.

Small Forward

The small forward is an extremely important player—he's the guy who can get baskets like a Shooting Guard, but has the driving power of a Power Forward. Finding a good Small Forward is not an easy task. Look for high rating in field goals, power, height, and blocked shots, in that order.

NFL QUARTERBACK CLUB '98
CHEATS AND CODES

Attributes Cheat

This helps you create better players. After you input the player's name, weight, height, etc, press **A** or **Start** to go to the "Attributes" screen. If you look at the big green gauge at the top of the screen, it isn't always filled all the way, so you have to reduce some things. If you want a better bar, press **B** to go back to the previous screen, then **A** again to return to the "Attributes" screen. The green bar will change. Keep doing this until you have the amount that you want.

Bonus Teams

For two bonus teams, simply enter the following code on the "Cheats" screen: **STNTXTM**.

Player Codes

Enter these codes at the cheats menu:

Code	Effect
bbmntbl	Tall and skinny players
crllwys	Jump farther
glythmd	Goliath mode
rnldswzngr	Stronger players
smlmdgt	Midget mode
jpnsmwr	Short and fat players
mchljnsn	Faster players
wltrpytn	Stronger Running Backs
bgbfyff	Stronger Receivers
downdrv	Improved secondary
gtnhnds	Fumble mode
sprslyd	Slippery field
dwndrv	Unlimited downs
brdwynmth	Makes all Quarterbacks stars

Play Through Injury

In *NFL Quarterback Club '98*, it's possible to make an injured man play on! This is particularly useful if a star player gets injured. Simply wait for the play to end, then immediately go to the

Substitution screen. Press the "Reset All" option and the injured player is back in the game! He'll be listed as injured, but will remain on the field. His stats won't suffer, either!

Speed Boost
To run faster, all you have to do is press **A** for a boost. You normally have to wait for the meter to build up again, but if you repeatedly tap the **A** button, the bar regenerates much more quickly and keeps your player running.

ROBOTRON 64
PASSWORDS

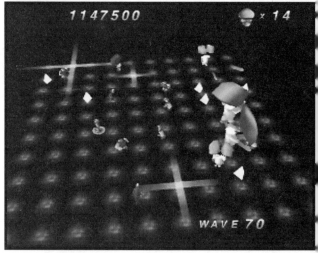

Level	Password	Level	Password
70	CQSCNLTBLG	130	FNJBLQCMKL
101	DJHFNQJBMJ	135	FQGDLQHMQL
110	DGHJLLLLDK	140	FNDJLGLMDM
115	DGTLLBRLKK	145	FLDLLQLMKM
120	DSJQLLSLRK	150	FQTNLBGMQM
125	DBDSLQCMDL	155	FJMTLBQLCN

CHEATS
● The following codes should be input on the set-up menu before you start the game.
50 Extra Lives
Up, Up, Down, Down, Left, Right, Left, Right, C(L), C(R), C(L), C(R)

Game Boy Mode

Up, Down, Right, C(L), Down, Up, Left, C(R), Up, Down

● These codes are entered while playing the game.

Flame-Thrower

Down, Right, Down, Right, C(R)

Four-Way Fire

Down, Down, Up, C(R)

Radiation Spray

Up, Down, C(R), C(L)

Shield

Down, Left, C(L), C(R)

Speed Up

Left, Left, Right, Right, C(U)

Three-Way Fire

Right, Right, C(L), C(D)

Two-Way Fire

Up, C(U), Up, C(U)

SAN FRANCISCO RUSH
CHEATS AND HIDDEN EXTRAS

Special Car

Win a circuit. From then on, if you're using the same player, you can press **Z** four times in a row on the "Track Select" screen to enable the Special car— Formula One.

Burnt Out Demo

Finish a game, crashing your car into a burnt-out wreck, then after "Game Over" starts flashing (but before it stops), hold down the **Left shoulder, Right shoulder**, and **Z** buttons until the post-game high score display demo begins. Your car will still be crashed and burning, but driving around the track as if nothing was wrong!

Skate Park

At the beginning of Track Four, there is an area to your left in which you can do lots of stunts. Use this for practice for the death-defying jumps you have to make—and just for fun!

Mine Cones

In this mode, all the traffic cones become huge land mines and blow up your car if you hit them. To activate this, go to the "Setup" screen and press: **Left shoulder, Right shoulder, Left shoulder, Right shoulder, Left shoulder, Right shoulder**.

Upside-Down Track

You can play the entire game upside down if you wish! Again, go to the "Setup" screen and press: **Up, Right, Down, Left, Down, Right, Up, Left** on the D-pad.

Foggy Night

Is the game still too easy for you on Extreme mode? Try racing on a foggy night by holding down all four **C** buttons as you select the fog intensity on the "Options" screen.

Car Mines

For a really interesting race, you can turn all the cars into landmines. This also activates the landmine traffic cones. If you run into a mine car, you blow up! On the "Car Select" screen press: **C(R), C(R), Z, C(D), C(U), Z, C(L), C(L)**.

No Game Timer

You can effectively have infinite time in your races by going to the "Setup" screen, holding **Z** and pressing: **C(D)-C(U), C(U)-C(D)**.

Weird Mode

You can really impress your friends with this cheat—it turns the game into a weird psychedelic experience by switching off all the textures used on the cars, track, and buildings. Go to the "Setup" screen again and press: **C(R)-Left, Z, C(R)-Left, Z**, where the directions are on the D-pad.

Change Gravity

For a bit of fun, or to make it easier to collect those hard-to-reach keys, you can alter the gravity in the game, making the cars bounce around a little more. Go to the "Setup" screen and press: **Z-Up, Z-Down, Up, Down, Up, Down**.

Change Car Size

You can even change the height of the car itself! Cycle from ultra-thin to big and chunky by pressing: **C(D)-C(U), C(U)-C(D)**.

Cycling Random High Score Names
Hit **Left, Right, Left, Right, Left, Right, Left, Right** on the
"Fast Times" or "Best Laps" records screens when they are
showing "Totals." Any unused entries in the list (which would
normally be filled with default names and scores) will cycle
randomly.

Auto Abort Disable
If you stray too far off the beaten track or come to a stop in a
normal game, the computer automatically puts you back where
you should be. This can be annoying when searching for hidden
keys, so you can disable it by going to the "Setup" screen and
pressing: **C(U), C(U), C(U), C(U)**.

Change Tire Size
You can pump up both the front and back tires on your car by
selecting your favorite vehicle on the "Car Select" screen then
pressing:
C(L)-C(R), C(R)-C(L) for front tires.
C(R)-C(L), C(L)-C(R) for back tires.
You have to perform these combinations repeatedly to cycle
through the various tire sizes.

Change Fog Color
Last, but not least, why not change the color of the fog, too?! You
can cycle from red to blue, to yellow, to pink, if you wish! This
guarantees a strange racing experience—especially if you have
maximum fog selected! On the "Car Select" screen hold **Z** and
press: **C(D), C(D), C(D)**.

TOP GEAR RALLY
SHORTCUTS

Track 1: Coastline

Immediately after the opening straightaway, you're faced with a choice: go ahead and through the tunnel, or take the road to the right. Go right, as this proves to be by far the easier route and can save you anything up to five seconds!

Now follow the track until you approach another tunnel. When you're safely through, the road turns right, then left. As you bear left, look at the fence on the outside edge of the corner—you should notice a break. Steer through the gap and continue to drive straight across a beach. This is the first shortcut.

Before long you get back onto the track proper. Follow the road left, right, then left again. As the course goes back to the right, you should notice a small break in the stone wall on your left—there's a white lighthouse in the background behind it. Drive through the break in the wall and across the field.

This is a big shortcut and gives you the opportunity to move swiftly up the rankings. Keep driving ahead and you're led back onto the track. The road passes through another short tunnel before the circuit is completed.

Track 2: The Jungle

Once the race is underway, move your car to the far right-hand side of the track and stay there as you make the first turn. Before you complete the turn, you should notice a small wooden hut in the background to the right. At this point, hit the brakes and swing the car to the right. You'll go through a small gap in the fence and enter a shortcut section that takes you through a small cave.

When you're back on the main track, you have to turn to the left then sharply to the right—both are signposted so watch out for the early warning! You enter a long left-hand turn that has a stone wall on the right-hand side (this is indicted by a row of arrows on the outside edge of the bend). As you approach the end of this corner, you should notice a break in the wall directly ahead of you. Drive at this, onto a grassy hill.

As you drive through the small shortcut area, you should

gradually turn your car to the right. This prevents you from dropping off the shortcut, back onto the track below. If you make a mistake, you won't get the full benefit of this shortcut, plus the subsequent crash decreases your speed.

Now just follow the sequence of easy turns back to the starting line.

Track 3: The Desert

As you leave the city behind you, look for a small house on the right-hand side of the road. Here you should slow down to approximately 60mph and drive onto the grass found just before the house itself. This is the first shortcut of the race, and it's also one of the most difficult to negotiate. If you're unsure of your driving ability, you would be well advised to ignore this shortcut until you have learned how to control your car more skillfully.

Next the track winds its way through a short valley, so be careful and watch out for the walls. Now you have a choice of route—do you take the high road or the low one? You should use the lower of the two then jam the accelerator to the floor, as this section is fast! The high road features a twisting series of sharp corners that really slow you down; the route you should have chosen only has one long, sweeping left-hander. From here it should be plain sailing to return to the opening straightaway and complete the lap.

Track 4: Mountain

After a long straightaway, the track becomes nothing more than a dirt road, so watch your handling of the car in this area, as the steering can be very jittery. After a sequence of sharp lefts and rights, you should see a sign on the right-hand side. It indicates that the track is about to fork off and you must quickly decide which route you wish to take.

Take the left-hand path but slow down to about 50 mph. This may seem extremely slow, but it's necessary if you want to use the following shortcut. When you're on the left-hand road, you should see a "jacked up road" sign. Head down here for the shortcut.

Be very careful and don't take this shortcut too fast or you'll crash. You don't need to go fast anyway, as the shortcut takes out a large section of the course—enough to make up four or even five places! Once you're back on the main section of the track, it's simply a case of making the easy turns until you reach the finish.

Track 5: Strip Mine

This final track is the toughest of the entire racing season. Follow these tips and use the shortcuts to give yourself a fighting chance of winning. Not long after the starting straightaway, look ahead for a fork in the road—it's time to decide your route! Take the right then follow the road until you can see an open mine, where the shortcut begins.

Drive into the mine tunnel then stay as tight to the right-hand wall as possible. You will reach a ramp that you should use to launch yourself onto a higher section of the underground mine. This is a tricky jump to make, so keep your speed high and stay close to the right-hand wall, as this gives you the best angle to make the jump.

CHEATS

Alternate Colors

To change the color of your vehicle, highlight it, then hold down the **Left** and **Right shoulder** buttons, plus all four of the **C** buttons! Now pushing **Up** or **Down** on the control pad changes your car's color. Pushing **Up** makes your car white, while pushing **Down** has the opposite effect, painting your vehicle black!

Chrome Plating

If you finish the fifth year, a new "Easter egg" allows you to change your car texture to a really cool mirror-type effect! Simply click any of the **C** buttons while you're on the vehicle selection screen to get a dazzling chrome finish.

Bonus Cars

The only way to access bonus vehicles is to do it the hard way and finish all of the races. Finishing the first year lets you drive a milk truck. The second year gives you the Helmet car, in the third you earn the Cuppa, and finally, the Beachball car is your reward for completing the fourth year. You exit the mine and drive back onto the road. Continue along the main route until you see a small house with a parking lot nearby. Stay on the right-hand side of the track and head down the very narrow dirt section ahead. You'll find a ramp that allows you to jump onto a section of road that is otherwise inaccessible.

From this point, the shortcut rejoins that main track just before the finish line! If you use these shortcuts to their maximum potential, you can almost guarantee yourself second or even first place, which is an excellent effort on such a difficult track.

Completion Date
On the title screen, hold down all four **C** buttons. A date is displayed at the top of the screen—this is the official completion date for the *Top Gear Rally* game.

'PlayStation' Mode
While playing the game press the following buttons: **B, Left, Right, Up, Left, Z and Right**. This removes all the texture filtering in the game, giving it a pixelated look, similar to that of a PlayStation game.

Rainbow Mode
While playing, press **C(D), Z, B, Up, Up, Right**. The road, backgrounds, and even the cars are painted with a rainbow of vivid colors.

View Different Credits
Go to the Options screen and click on the Credits icon. Now as they start to run, quickly press **Left, C(D), Right, Down**, and

finally the **Z** button. You return to the Options menu, where the Credits medallion will have an "R" on it. Click again to view the alternative credits!

WAYNE GRETZKY HOCKEY '98
ICE HOCKEY BASICS

● Once you lose the puck, concentrate on regaining position as quickly as possible, as this prevents your opponent getting close to your goal. Getting the puck back quickly has another advantage: The longer you chase around after it, the more tired your defensemen become, and in a long game this is an important factor. If you reach the third period and find that your number one defensive line is too tired to play, you're putting yourself under unnecessary pressure. Getting the puck back and keeping it means the opposing team has tired defensemen instead.

● If you're playing in Arcade mode, you can choose which rules, if any, are effective during the match. This means that you can concentrate on honing your skills, instead of worrying about whether you have fouled an opponent or committed an icing! This is very useful when you're relatively new to the game, as constant calls for icing, off-sides, and the like can be very frustrating when all you want to do is get on with the match and practice your hockey! Once you have the hang of things, you can turn the rules back on, then begin to really play the game!

CHEATS & CODES

Bonus Teams

On the Options screen, hold the Left shoulder button then press **C(R), C(L), C(L), C(R), C(L), C(L), C(R), C(L), C(L)**. If you have been successful, a "1" appears on the 10th spot from the left. You now have access to Minnesota, Quebec, Winnipeg, and Hartford.

Choose Your Opponent

This is useful if you feel like playing an easy game against a weak CPU team. Simply highlight the team you wish to play against, then press the **C(R)** button three times. You should hear a click that tells you the cheat has worked.

Debug Mode

When you're on the Options screen, press the **C(D)** and **Right shoulder** buttons together, then **C(L)** and **Right shoulder** together. A screen appears where you can alter the first six bits of a computer register.

To alter the players' features , use these controls:

C(D)+Right shoulder: Changes head size
C(L)+Right shoulder: Changes body size
C(U)+Right shoulder: Changes height

Here are a few examples to get you started:

100000	Stocky players
010000	Stocky players, big heads
110000	Stocky players, small heads
001000	Small players, small announcer
000100	Large players, large announcer
000010	Crunched players, small announcer
000001	Elongated players, large announcer
110110	Large players, small heads, large announcer
010010	Crunched players, large heads, small announcer
010101	Large players, large heads, large announcer
010001	Elongated players, large heads, large announcer

View Sponsors
Simply press **Z** while in the Options, Setup, or Audio menus. The names of all the sponsors will scroll along the bottom of the screen.

WCW VS. NWO WORLD TOUR
SPECIAL MOVES

LEX LUGER

Crown Chop	Tap B close
Knee Kick	Tap B far
Chest Slap	U+Tap B close
Mid Kick	U+Tap B far
Spinning Roundhouse	Hold B
Drop Kick	U+Hold B
Crown Bamboochop	Tap A+A
Super Elbow	Tap A+U+A
Body Slam	Tap A+D+A
Hiplock Takedown	Tap A+B
Skyscraper Backdrop	Tap A+U+B
Hold Tombstone	Tap A+D+B

STING

Forearm Elbow	Tap B close
Knee Kick	Tap B far
Knuckle Strike	U+Tap B close
Stomach Kick	U+Tap B far
Soccer Kick	Hold B
Stinger Punch	U+Hold B
1-Hand Hammer	Tap A+A
Shoulder Drop	Tap A+U+A
Body Slam	Tap A+D+A
Headlock Takedown	Tap A+B
Lifting Slam	Tap A+U+B

Back Buster .... Tap A+D+B
Scorpion Death Drop .... Hold A+A
Belly to Belly Suplex .... Hold A+U+A
Power Bomb .... Hold A+D+A
Face Crusher .... Hold A+B
Stinger Slam .... Hold A+U+B
Small Package Press .... Hold A+D+B

GIANT

Clubbing Forearm .... Tap B close
Big Boot .... Tap B far
Ham Bone .... U+Tap B close
Stomach Stuff .... U+Tap B far
Head Kick .... Hold B
Super Kick .... U+Hold B
Head Butt .... Tap A+A
Giant Forearm .... Tap A+U+A
Body Slam .... Tap A+D+A
Elbow Crank .... Tap A+B
Standing Press Throw .... Tap A+U+B
Leg Sweep .... Tap A+D+B
Top Rope Clothesline .... Hold A+A
Overhead Rack .... Hold A+U+A
Double Arm Power Bomb .... Hold A+D+A
Knee Crusher Crash .... Hold A+B
Choke Hold .... Hold A+U+B
Pile Driver .... Hold A+D+B

SCOTT STEINER

Elbow to Head .... Tap B close
Knee Kick .... Tap B far
Chest Slap .... U+Tap B close
Ricky Kick .... U+Tap B far
Drop Kick .... Hold B
Linebacker Lift .... U+Hold B
Forearm Smash .... Tap A+A
Fireman's Carry .... Tap A+U+A
Shoulder Tackle .... Tap A+D+A
Gut Wrench Suplex .... Tap A+B
Snap Suplex .... Tap A+U+B
Shoulder Breaker .... Tap A+D+B
Speedy Side Suplex .... Hold A+A

Belly to Belly Suplex........................Hold A+U+A
Stud Driver Bomb ....Hold A+D+A
Front Suplex....................................Hold A+B
Belly to Back Suplex........................Hold A+U+B
Screwdriver Power Slam ....Hold A+D+B

RICK STEINER

Rough Elbow.....................................Tap B close
Knee Kick ....Tap B far
Hammer Punch..................................U+Tap B close
Soccer Kick ....U+Tap B far
Shoulder Smash.................................Hold B
Bulldog Forearm................................U+Hold B
Bull Elbow ....Tap A+A
Bulldog Smash....................................Tap A+U+A
Lift Slam..Tap A+D+A
Neck Holding Throw ....Tap A+B
Shoulder Press Slam.........................Tap A+U+B
Shoulder Buster ....Tap A+D+B
Back Breaker......................................Hold A+A
Steinerline..Hold A+U+A
German Suplex...................................Hold A+D+A
Belly to Belly Suplex.........................Hold A+B
Overhead Press ....Hold A+U+B
Canadian Backbreaker ....Hold A+D+B

RIC FLAIR

Straight Fist..Tap B close
Kick...Tap B far
Throat Chop ....U+Tap B close
Knee Kick ....U+Tap B far
Roundhouse ....Hold B
Drop Kick...U+Hold B
Flair Punch...Tap A+A
Forearm Smash..................................Tap A+U+A
Snap Mare ....Tap A+D+A
Elbow Smash ....Tap A+B
Suplex ....Tap A+U+B
Pile Driver ....Tap A+D+B
Flying Major.......................................Hold A+A
Revolution Takedown.......................Hold A+U+A
Brain Buster ....Hold A+D+A

Manhattan Drop...............................Hold A+B
Canadian Back Breaker....................Hold A+U+B
Small Package Press..........................Hold A+D+B

ULTIMO DRAGON

Karate Punch.....................................Tap B close
Karate Kick..Tap B far
Karate Chop ....U+Tap B close
Spinning Kick....................................U+Tap B far
Drop Kick..Hold B
Rev Spinning Drop Kick.....................U+Hold B
Cancun Punch...................................Tap A+A
Snap Mare...Tap A+U+A
Body Drop Takedown ....Tap A+D+A
Armwhip Elbow................................Tap A+B
Snap Suplex ....Tap A+U+B
Ultimodriver......................................Tap A+D+B
Side Suplex ....Hold A+A
Vertical Brain Buster.........................Hold A+U+A
Tombstone..Hold A+D+A
Drop DDT..Hold A+B
Belly to Back Suplex.........................Hold A+U+B
Grapple Doctor Bomb ....Hold A+D+B

DEAN MALENKO

Body Blow ....Tap B close
Sharp Low Kick ....Tap B far
Hooked Slap......................................U+Tap B close
Middle Kick.......................................U+Tap B far
Low Drop Kick...................................Hold B
High Drop Kick..................................U+Hold B
Forearm Smash.................................Tap A+A
Snap Mare...Tap A+U+A
Body Slam...Tap A+D+A
Reverse Arm Bar...............................Tap A+B
Bryant Suplex....................................Tap A+U+B
Pile Driver ....Tap A+D+B
Atomic Crush ....Hold A+A
Missile Drop......................................Hold A+U+A
Torpedo...Hold A+D+A
Express Brain Buster.........................Hold A+B
Small Package Press..........................Hold A+D+B

EDDY GUERRERO

Uppercut	Tap B close
Mid Kick	Tap B far
Straight Punch	U+Tap B close
Knee Kick	U+Tap B far
Super Kick	Hold B
Drop Kick	U+Hold B
Face Rip	Tap A+A
Snap Mare	Tap A+U+A
Body Slam	Tap A+D+A
Arm Drag Smash	Tap A+B
Snap Suplex	Tap A+U+B
Shoulder Breaker	Tap A+D+B
Overhead Toss	Hold A+A
Tombstone Suplex	Hold A+U+A
Blockbuster	Hold A+D+A
Belly to Back Suplex	Hold A+B
Pendulum Backbreaker	Hold A+U+B
Power Bomb	Hold A+D+B

REY MYSTERIO, JR.

Forearm Punch	Tap B close
Reverse Kick	Tap B far
Kenpo Punch	U+Tap B close
Mid Kick	U+Tap B far
Spinning Rev Drop Kick	Hold B
Drop Kick	U+Hold B
Forearm Smash	Tap A+A
Snap Mare	Tap A+U+A
Falling Arm-Drag	Tap A+D+A
Elbow Grease	Tap A+B
Cyclone Spin	Tap A+U+B
Screwdriver Slam	Tap A+D+B
Spinning Foot Lock	Hold A+A
Shoulder Flip Press	Hold A+U+A
Break Dance Flip	Hold A+D+A
Suplex Press	Hold A+B
Booty Bomb	Hold A+U+B
Small Package Press	Hold A+D+B

CHRIS BENOIT

Body Elbow	Tap B close
Knee Kick	Tap B far
Chest Slap	U+Tap B close
Karate Kick	U+Tap B far
Shoulder Charge	Hold B
Drop Kick	U+Hold B
Flying Forearm	Tap A+A
Head Butt	Tap A+U+A
Super Slam	Tap A+D+A
Spinal Elbow	Tap A+B
Snap Suplex	Tap A+U+B
Cross-Arm Suplex	Tap A+D+B
Gut Wrench Suplex	Hold A+A
Twist Back Drop	Hold A+U+A
Reverse Face Buster	Hold A+D+A
Standing Clothesline	Hold A+B
Belly to Belly Press	Hold A+U+B
Power Bomb Press	Hold A+D+B

STEVEN REGAL

Peasant Slap	Tap B close
Mid Kick	Tap B far
Peon Punch	U+Tap B close
Low Kick	U+Tap B far
Drop Kick	Hold B
Reverse Kick	U+Hold B
Uppercut Forearm	Tap A+A
Snap Mare	Tap A+U+A
Body Slam	Tap A+D+A
Hiplock Takedown	Tap A+B
Neck Breaker	Tap A+U+B
Holding Arm Bar	Tap A+D+B
Chicken Wing Suplex	Hold A+A
Regal Suplex	Hold A+U+A
Shoulder Slide Press	Hold A+D+A
Belly to Belly Suplex	Hold A+B
Twisted Wrist Throw	Hold A+U+B
Regal Roll	Hold A+D+B

YOSHI'S STORY
THE GOOD GUYS

Baby Yoshis

Each Yoshi has a favorite color in the game—it's usually the same color as his skin. You need to think about the favorite color of the Yoshi you choose as you play, and change your attack patterns accordingly. Shy Guys, for example, come in all colors and change color when Yoshi uses his Hip Drop move onto the ground nearby. Eating a Shy Guy that's any old color gives one measly point, but eating one in Yoshi's favorite color gives three points!

The same scoring system works for fruit, too. If you dash through each level, eating any fruit that comes to hand (or tongue!), you won't score highly at all. You must be selective, eating only the favorite fruit of your Yoshi first, then the lucky fruit of the day. If you need more fruit to complete the level when other sources have been exhausted, you can start eating anything.

Green Yoshi
Favorite color: Green
Favorite fruit: Watermelon
Pink Yoshi
Favorite color: Red
Favorite fruit: Apple
Red Yoshi
Favorite color: Red
Favorite fruit: Apple
Yellow Yoshi
Favorite color: Yellow
Favorite fruit: Banana
Blue Yoshi
Favorite color: Purple
Favorite fruit: Grapes
Purple Yoshi
Favorite color: Purple
Favorite fruit: Grapes

Miss Warp

You will find four Miss
Warps in every level of
Yoshi's Story. As Yoshi
roams around, they're found
lying on the ground, fast
asleep. By jumping on their
heads Yoshi can wake them,
triggering a restart point. If
Yoshi loses a life, he goes back to the last Miss Warp he woke
instead of the start of the level. Miss Warps are also useful for
moving around each world at lightning speed. By standing on
them and pressing **Up** on the joystick, Yoshi warps between the
Miss Warps he has already awakened.

Poochy

This friendly little dog is Yoshi's pal and can be found yapping on
various levels. There is more to this dog than first meets the eye—
set him free or follow him and wait for the little dog to stop and
bark. He's trying to tell Yoshi that there's something secret nearby.
Use the **R** button to sniff around near Poochy and if you have the
right spot, Yoshi leaps up and down with joy! Use a Hip Drop on the
secret spot to reveal what's hidden—usually melons or coins.

THE BAD GUYS

Shy Guys

These are the most common enemies that Yoshi encounters, and
also happen to be the favorite food of the little dinosaurs. They
come in a rainbow of colors—eating the ones that are the same
color as your Yoshi will put a big smile on his face!

There are also two hidden Shy Guys, one white and one black.
The white one is a turncoat and joins Yoshi in his adventure, helping
out where he can. The black Shy Guy is found by picking up a black
egg then exiting the level
with it.

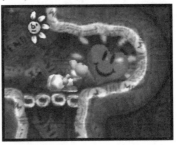

Baby Koopa

If you have played *Super
Mario 64*, you'll know all
about King Koopa, the evil
creature who is out to get
Mario. Well, in *Yoshi's Story*, it's

his youngest offspring we have to contend with—Baby Koopa! He looks similar to his dad, with a striking green shell and red face, but isn't quite as fearsome. Yoshi encounters Koopa at the end of his adventures, and must kill him to finish the game.

PICKING UP POINTS

Playing *Yoshi's Story* successfully is all a matter of collecting points. Any shmuck can complete the game, eating any of the fruits along the way, but they will end up with a minuscule score. You must learn and understand the scoring system, then use it to build up the biggest score possible.

Scores are calculated as a total of six categories:

1. Fruits
Any fruit 1 point
Favorite fruit or melon 3 points
Lucky fruit 8 points
Heart fruit 8 points
Each level is completed by eating 30 fruits. The score you can earn for these varies dramatically, depending on the way you eat them. Chomping on the same type of fruit in a row multiplies the scores you can earn each time. A lucky fruit, for example, is worth eight points, but eating six in a row gives 168 points (8 × [1+2+3+4+5+6] = 168).

The lucky fruit is determined before you start, in a simple roulette game. The fruits will cycle and pressing the A button stops the roulette on your lucky fruit.

2. Enemies
Eating a colored enemy 1 point
Killing a colored enemy 2 points
Eating a favorite colored enemy 3 points
Killing a favorite colored enemy 6 points
Yoshi can defeat his enemies in three different ways. First, he can use his tongue to lap them up and swallow them. Each one swallowed makes Yoshi lay an egg, which he can then use as a weapon. Swallowing enemies in your Yoshi's favorite color gives

more points than the others. Secondly, he can perform a Hip Drop on their heads, squashing them flat. Finally, the eggs collected can be used as weapons to kill enemies. The Hip Drop and egg throw methods earn you double the points, so

these are recommended. You can create even greater scores if you line up rows of enemies before firing an egg at them. Killing multiple enemies with a single egg multiplies the score each time, first x4, then x8, then x16. For example, killing off five Shy Guys in a line with an egg, the third one being in Yoshi's favorite color, give this score: 1x2 + 1x4 + 3x8 + 1x16 + 1x16 = 62 points. Eating them all would give this score: 1+1+3+1+1 = 7 points!

3. Coins
Gold coin 1 point
Every platform game must have its throwaway collectibles, and in *Yoshi's Story* it's the Nintendo favorite, gold coins. Each coin collected gives one point, so they're not too important to collect for a high score. We recommend you pick up every single one you see, though—some reveal secrets when collected that you will otherwise miss.

4. Special hearts
Special heart 100 points

These are giant red hearts that sway backward and forward. Being so special, you can bet they are hidden away in the farthest reaches of Yoshi's storybook—and there are three to collect in every level. They not only give 100 points, they also open up new levels on the next page of the storybook.

5. Melons
Each melon 100 points

These juicy fruit are the most important items to collect. Each one picked up earns 100 points, in addition to any points picked up in point one. Every level has 30 of them, many hidden away in secret locations. Collect all melons in a level and your score will rocket!

6. Remaining Yoshis
Each Yoshi left on completing level 100 points

You start the game with six Yoshis, all vying for your affections. Each time you miss a platform and fall off the screen or run out of life flower, you lose a Yoshi and must select another. At the end of each level, you get 100 points for every Yoshi remaining. It's always good to know what to expect before you jump in with your size ten feet. Here is a brief description of each world and level in Yoshi's Story, complete with many of the special heart locations!

LIFE

Nintendo has come up with an ingenious method of keeping track of energy in Yoshi's Story—a life flower! The flower sits in the top-left corner of the screen at all times and has eight petals. There are various things Yoshi can do to affect the number of petals on the flower:

Eating lucky fruit +8 petals
Eating favorite colored enemy +3 petals
Eating favorite fruit or melon +3 petals
Eating other fruit +1 petal
Eating red pepper -1 petal
Hit by enemy -3 petals
Eating a bad-tasting enemy -1 petal

GAMESHARK CODES
AEROFIGHTERS ASSAULT
Infinite Chaffs 8027e017000a
Infinite Special Weapons 8027e4d20002

AUTOMOBILI LAMBORGHINI
Infinite Time..800ce76f0063
100 Points 800ce7430064
Extra Vehicles 800985c30001
Extra Vehicles 800985c50001
Extra Vehicles 800985c70001
Extra Vehicles 800985cb0001
Extra Vehicles 800985cd0001
Extra Vehicles 800985cf0001

BOMBERMAN 64
Infinite Lives...802ac6270063
Stop Timer 802ac6430000
Infinite Credits...802ac62b0063
Gems...802ac62f0063
Battle Mode In The Gutter Stage.............802ac61f0006
Battle Mode In The Gutter Stage.............802ac7030006
Battle Mode Sea Sick Stage 802ac61f0007
Battle Mode Sea Sick Stage 802ac7030007
Battle Mode Blizzard Battle Stage............802ac61f0008
Battle Mode Blizzard Battle Stage............802ac7030008
Battle Mode Lost At Sea Stage 802ac61f0009
Battle Mode Lost At Sea Stage 802ac7030009

CHAMELEON TWIST
Extra Crowns..8025176700l5
Access All Levels 8020850e00ff
Access All Levels 80208510 00ff

CLAYFIGHTER 63 1/3
Extra Characters/Secret Options 801a2b41000f

CRUIS'N USA
Always Place 1st...8015022b0001
Unlimited Time 8015094d0045

DARK RIFT

Enable Demitron	80049df40001
Enable Sonork	80049df00001

DOOM 64

Always Have BFG 9000	800632db0001
Always Have Chain Gun	800632cf0001
Always Have Chainsaw	800632bb0001
Always Have Double Shotgun	800632cb0001
Always Have Gun	800632c30001
Always Have Missile Launcher	800632d30001
Always Have Plasma Rifle	800632d70001
Always Have Shotgun	800632c70001
Blue Key	8006328f0001
Blue Skull Key	8006329b0001
Gun/Chain Gun Ammo	800632e300ff
Invincible	8006330b0002
Missile Ammo	800632ef0064
Plasma/BFG/Weapons Ammo	800632eb0064
Red Key	800632970001
Red Skull Key	800632a30001
Shotgun Ammo	800632e70064
Yellow Key	800632930001
Yellow Skull Key	8006329f0001

DUKE NUKEM 64

Cheat Menu	801012d80001
Cheat Menu	801012dc0001
Cheat Menu	801012e00001
Cheat Menu	801012e40001
Cheat Menu	801012e80001
Expander/Missile Launcher	812a5ac00101
Have All Keys	802a5a47000f
Infinite Armor	8024746300ff
Infinite Expander Ammo	802a5a0d00ff
Infinite Grenades	802a5a0700ff
Infinite Jet Pack	812a5a8e0640
Infinite Laser Trip Bomb Ammo	802a5a1300ff
Infinite Missiles	802a5a0f00ff
Infinite Pipe Bomb Ammo	802a5a0900ff
Infinite Plasma Ammo	802a5a1100ff
Infinite Shrinker Ammo	802a5a0b00ff

Infinite SMG Ammo 802a5a0500ff
Pipe Bombs/Shrinker..............................812a5abe0101
Plasma Cannon/Laser Trip Bombs............812a5ac20101
SMGs/Grenade Launcher..........................812a5abc0101

EXTREME-G

100 Points 80167c370063
Anti-Grav + Fish Eye Lens.........................80095f6f000a
Anti-Gravity Mode.....................................80095f6f0008
Boulder Mode...80095f6f0001
Boulder Mode + Fish Eye Lens.................80095f6f0003
Boulder Mode + Wireframe Mode..........80095f6f0011
Extreme Mode..80095f6e0002
Fish Eye Lens...80095f6f0002

FIFA SOCCER 64

Home Team Scores 0.................................801190470000
Away Team Scores 0...................................801190430000
Home Team Scores 9.................................801190470009
Away Team Scores 9...................................801190430009

GOLDENEYE 007

2XGrenade Launchers...............................8006966e0001
2XHunting Knife 800696710001
2XLaser..800696720001
2XRC-P90..8006966f0001
2XRocket Launchers..................................8006966d0001
2XThrowing Knife 800696700001
All Guns 800696530001
Bond Invisible..8006965a0001
DK Mode...8006965c0001
Enemy Rockets 8006966c0001
Fast Animation 8006966a0001
Gold PP7...800696650001
Golden Gun..800696630001
Infinite Ammo 8006965b0001
Invincible 800696520001
Laser...800696620001
Line Mode...800696570001
Magnum 800696610001
No Radar (Multi)..800696670001
Paint Ball Mode..8006965f0001

Silver PP7 800696640001
Slow Animation 8006966b0001
Tiny Bond 8006965e0001
Turbo Mode 800696680001

MACE: THE DARK AGE
Extra Characters 8007f9f80001
Infinite Health P1 ....8008b1e70064
Infinite Health P2 ....8008ae5f0064
No Health P1 ....8008b1e70000
No Health P2 ....8008ae5f0000
Z Trigger Deathblow P1 ....d007cd2a0020
Z Trigger Deathblow P1 ....8008ae5f0000
R Button Health Restore P1 ....d007cd2b0010
R Button Health Restore P1 ....8008b1e70064

MARIO KART 64
No Laps to Race 811643900000
No Laps to Race 811643920002

MORTAL KOMBAT MYTHOLOGIES: SUB-ZERO
Infinite Lives 8010bcff0005

MULTI RACING CHAMPIONSHIP
Infinite Time 80094e970064
Infinite Time d0094e97000a
Low Course Time 8009483b0000
Always Place 1st 800a960f0000

SAN FRANCISCO RUSH
GS Button for Extra Track 881000500006
Auto Abort Disable 800f40780001
Change Textures 800f3da00001
Cones to Mines 800f3f880001
No Collisions 800f40500001
Resurrect In Place 800f40800001
Stop Timer 800f40900001
Upside Down Mode 800f40610001
Flat Cars 800f40b10001
Fat Cars 800f40b10002
Giant Cars 800f40b10003

STAR FOX 64

Hyper Laser...8015791b0002
Infinite Armor 8013ab2700ff
Infinite Armor 80137c4700ff
Loads O' Hits..8015790b00ff
Unlimited Lives P1 801579110040
Unlimited Smart Bombs P1 ....8016dc130004

STAR WARS SHADOWS OF THE EMPIRE

Unlimited Lives..800e05cb00ff
Unlimited Missiles.......................................800e126500ff

TOP GEAR RALLY

Extra Tracks..813243ceffff
Extra Vehicles 813243ccffff
Level 1 Points...8032431f0064
Level 2 Points...803243210064
Level 3 Points...803243230064
Level 4 Points...803243250064
Level 5 Points...803243270064
Level 6 Points...803243290064

WAR GODS

Unlimited Time...8033f31b0063
Cheat Menu...803365930001

WCW VS. NWO

Infinite Time..800f16ef0000
Extra Characters...8006066500ff
Maximum Spirit P1 ....800f08010064
No Spirit P1 ....800f08010000
Maximum Spirit P2 ....800f0ba10064
No Spirit P2 ....800f0ba10000

WHEEL OF FORTUNE

Extra Cash P1 ....810b9992ffff

GameShark™

This is not a game.

It's a game enhancer.

Plug it in

and turn it on.

Reveal the hidden.

Unleash the fury.

Feed on weakness.

and never die.

INTERACT

Abuse the Power.